Discover JOHN

THE WORD BECAME FLESH

by
Brent and Diane Averill

FAITH
ALIVE®
Christian Resources

Grand Rapids, Michigan

MW01102289

Unless otherwise noted, Scripture quotations in this publication are from
the HOLY BIBLE, NEW INTERNATIONAL VERSION, © 1973, 1978, 1984,
International Bible Society. Used by permission of Zondervan Bible
Publishers.

Cover photo: Corbis

The authors wish to acknowledge with thanks that in preparing their
manuscript for this study they drew on some ideas for discussion questions
and responses from two earlier studies produced in the Discover Your Bible
series: *Discover Jesus in John: Who He Is* by Sylvia Boomsma (1992),
and *Discover Jesus in John: The Lives He Touched* by Edith Bajema (1992).
All rights reserved by Faith Alive Christian Resources.

Discover Your Bible series. *Discover John: The Word Became Flesh* (Leader
Guide), © 2005 by Faith Alive Christian Resources, 2850 Kalamazoo Ave. SE,
Grand Rapids, MI 49560. All rights reserved. With the exception of brief
excerpts for review purposes, no part of this book may be reproduced in any
manner whatsoever without written permission from the publisher. Printed
in the United States of America on recycled paper.

We welcome your comments. Call us at 1-800-333-8300 or e-mail us at
editors@faithaliveresources.org.

ISBN 978-1-59255-224-5

10 9 8 7 6 5 4 3 2

Jewish ruling council—see **Sanhedrin.**

Jews—descendants of the Israelite tribes of Judah and Benjamin who returned from exile in Babylon to rebuild Jerusalem and the temple of the Lord after 538 B.C. The gospel writer John uses this term frequently, sometimes to refer to the Jewish people but most often to refer to the Jewish religious leaders in Jerusalem.

John the Baptist—the last prophet who called people to repentance to help them prepare for the coming of the Messiah. John baptized people in the Jordan River as a symbol of their repentance and preparation. John was also Jesus' cousin. (See Luke 1:5-66; 3:1-6, 15-20.)

John the disciple—a close friend and disciple of Jesus who wrote the gospel of John. He also wrote three letters and the book of Revelation in the New Testament. (See the Introduction to this study for additional background on John.)

Joseph—A favorite son of the patriarch Jacob. He was sold into slavery in Egypt by his brothers, but by God's grace he found favor with his masters and rose to become the second-highest ruler in Egypt. During a great famine he invited his family to move to Egypt, and they flourished there for many years, but eventually a new ruler came into power and enslaved them. The people of Israel remained slaves in Egypt for more than four hundred years, until God delivered them through the leadership of Moses (see Gen. 37-Ex. 12).

Lamb of God—John the Baptist used this phrase to describe Jesus at the time of his baptism as he began his public ministry (John 1:29, 35). This title implied that Jesus as Messiah would be a sacrificial substitute for sins (based on traditional sacrifices for Passover and atonement for sin—Ex. 12; Lev. 16; see also Heb. 10:1-18).

the Law (and the Prophets)—In Jesus' day people often used this term to refer to the body of Old Testament writings that made up the Jewish Scriptures (see Matt. 5:17; 22:40).

manna—a food that God provided for the Israelites during their travels in the desert after their release from slavery in Egypt. The manna appeared on the ground each morning, except on the Sabbath, and could be used for baking bread. Many of the Jews believed the Messiah would renew the sending of this "bread from heaven" (see John 6:32-35).

Messiah—the promised deliverer of God's people. Both the Hebrew word *Messiah* and the Greek word *Christ* mean "Anointed One." Through the prophets God promised to send the Messiah to deliver God's people from evil oppressors and to rule them in righteousness forever. The people misunderstood these promises, however, and looked for a

Messiah who would be a political ruler and gather an army to rout all their physical enemies. But as Jesus revealed through his work and teaching, the Messiah came to save God's people from the oppression of sin and death and to give them new life forever with God. He rules today in heaven at the right hand of the Father, and when he comes again at the end of time, he will fully establish God's everlasting kingdom of righteousness on earth. (See Matt. 26:63-64; John 16:5-16; 1 Cor. 15; Rev. 21:1-5; 22:1-5.)

money changers—officials who exchanged Roman currency into the Jewish currency acceptable to temple authorities for the payment of offerings and temple taxes.

Moses—the leader of the Israelites when God delivered them from slavery in Egypt and as they lived in the wilderness before entering the promised land (Palestine). Moses received the law from God and taught it to the Israelites.

Passover—This feast took place each spring to celebrate the Israelites' exodus from slavery in Egypt. The name commemorates God's protection of Israelite households during a final plague sent to convince the Egyptian king (pharaoh) to let the Israelites go. God promised that upon seeing the blood of a sacrificed lamb on the doorframes of a house, God would *pass over* that house and not allow the plague of death to take the life of the firstborn in that house (see Ex. 12).

Pharisees—an elite group that emphasized precise obedience to scriptural and traditional law. A number of Pharisees were part of the Sanhedrin, the Jewish ruling council.

priests—officials who served in the temple and belonged to the tribe of Levi; also often called Levites.

Pool of Siloam—a pool at the southern end of Jerusalem.

the Prophet—In Deuteronomy 18:15-19 Moses describes this person whom God promised to raise up to teach the people in the name of the Lord. While other great prophets such as Elijah, Isaiah, Jeremiah, and John the Baptist served God faithfully and filled this description in some ways, Jesus is the ultimate fulfillment of this promise.

rabbi—a Jewish religious scholar and teacher. Well-known rabbis often had disciples.

Sabbath—the seventh day of the week (Saturday), set aside as a day of rest and restoration according to the law of Moses. Jewish religious leaders developed a stringent code of rules for keeping the Sabbath, and Jesus often criticized them for being too legalistic in this regard (see Mark 2:23-3:6; Luke 13:10-17; John 5:16-17; 7:21-24).

- **How did "the One and Only" make God known?**

The one and only Son of God came to earth as one of us. He became human as Jesus Christ, our only Savior. Living with us, he revealed the character of God, showing us how to live for God. Dying in our place, he saved us from death. Rising to life again, he gives us new life so that we can begin, even now, to live for God, guided by the Holy Spirit. The remainder of our study of the book of John will fill in many details on how Jesus Christ reveals God and his amazing grace to us all.

Question for Reflection

If you were either John the disciple or John the Baptist, what would you say about the Word, Jesus?

Use this question to review important points from this study lesson. Remember that Jesus is God; he was involved in creating all things, became human for our sake, is the One and Only who reveals God to us all, and more. Invite group members to share what they have learned, and if they aren't certain they agree with everything covered, allow room for them to think and talk about the things we've touched on in these opening verses of John.

Also remember to pray for your group members, asking the Spirit of God to speak to their hearts and to help each one grow through this study of the gospel record.

Lesson 2

John 1:19-51

A Web of Connections

Additional Related Scriptures

Isaiah 40:3; 53:4-7	Mark 1:4, 9-11, 14-20
Malachi 3-4	Luke 3:21-22; 5:1-11
Matthew 3; 4:18-22	John 3:27-30

Introductory Notes

Our Scripture for this lesson gives us more information on the work of John the Baptist, helping us explore the testimony of John as he announces Jesus' mission. In this passage we meet some of John's disciples who become disciples of Jesus. We also see John modeling the statement he later makes about having to become less as Jesus becomes greater (John 3:30). Toward the end of John 1 it becomes clear that all who are introduced to Jesus are compelled to tell others about him, and we'll observe how the gospel spreads through a web of connections.

Optional Share Question

Have you ever connected two of your friends or played matchmaker? How did things turn out?

1. *John 1:19-23*

    a. *What were some of the Jewish leaders' mistaken notions about John, and how did he respond?*

When the priests and Levites came to ask John the Baptist who he was, he made clear that he was not the Messiah (Christ). (As a footnote in the NIV Bible explains, "'The Christ' [Greek] and 'the Messiah' [Hebrew] both mean 'the Anointed One.'")

Then the religious leaders asked John if he was Elijah. According to Malachi 3:1-5 and 4:5-6, God would send Elijah the prophet to precede the coming of the Messiah. John indicated that he was not Elijah (who incidentally was last seen across the Jordan River from Jericho many years before— 2 Kings 2:5-18). A text note in the *NIV Study Bible* adds, "When Jesus later said the Baptist was Elijah (Matt. 11:14; 17:10-13), he meant it in a sense that John was a fulfillment of the prophecy of Malachi 4:5" (see also Luke 1:17).

Finally, the leaders asked John if he was "the Prophet," and again he said no. This apparently was a reference to the great prophet mentioned in

Deuteronomy who would be like Moses and would tell the people what God wanted him to say (Deut. 18:15-19).

When the Jewish leaders finally asked, "Who are you?" John answered by quoting the prophet Isaiah: "I am the voice of one calling in the desert. 'Make straight the way for the Lord'" (see Isa. 40:3).

- **Why do you think these leaders were so curious about John?**

Throughout the past several hundred years of their history, ever since their exile to Babylon and even after their later return to their homeland, the Jews had longed for the promised Messiah to come and deliver them from their oppressors and set up a rule of righteousness (characterized by peace and justice) in their land (see 2 Chron. 36:15-23; Jer. 23:5-8). At the time of John's preaching ministry the Roman Empire ruled the land, and its tactics often involved cruel punishment, slavery, and heavy taxation to remind the people that Rome was in control. Many political zealots and self-proclaimed prophets tried staging rebellions in those days, so it was common for an upstart leader to stir up the people's hopes by claiming to be the Messiah.

In the meantime, the Jewish religious leaders developed political agreements with the Roman authorities, promising to help govern the people by their own laws while also receiving preferential treatment from Rome (favored social status and a grand temple in Jerusalem for their religious practices). In other words, the religious leaders had it pretty good and wanted to keep it that way. So when they heard of a new prophet or political zealot stirring up the people, it made sense to find out what that person was up to. If the person was a phony, they knew they needed to prevent a rebellion that could cost the lives of many people and threaten their own standing with the authorities. (See Matt. 27:62-28:15; Acts 5:33-39.)

While some of these religious leaders had good intentions and longed for the real Messiah to come (John 3:1-2; 19:38-39), many had closed their hearts and minds so that they wouldn't listen to the word of God as John preached it (Matt. 3:1-12; John 1:24-27). The fact that John was out in the desert talking like a prophet and wearing clothes like Elijah (made of camel's hair and with a leather belt—see 2 Kings 1:8; Matt. 3:4) was more than a little significant.

b. Why do you think John the Baptist used Scripture to describe who he was?

John used Scripture to show the religious leaders what his true purpose was. When the priests and Levites pressed him for an answer, he responded by quoting Isaiah 40:3, a verse that encourages God's people to prepare the way for the coming Messiah. Wherever a king traveled in ancient Israel, the people would clear the road ahead and make it smooth to show honor for their leader.

- **How did John fulfill Isaiah 40:3?**

John saw himself as the one who was preparing the way for the Messiah, and this called for repentance on the part of the people. The Messiah had to be received with a penitent spirit, not a proud or self-righteous attitude like many of the religious leaders had (Mal. 3:1-2; 4:1-2; Matt. 3:7-12).

In Malachi 3:7 the Lord says, "Ever since the time of your forefathers you have turned away from my decrees and have not kept them. Return to me, and I will return to you." The word *repent* means "turn around" or "turn back." By calling the people to repentance, John the Baptist was telling them to turn back, to return to the Lord, just as Malachi and Isaiah and many other prophets had done (see Isa. 1:4-6, 11-20; Jer. 18:11).

2. *John 1:24-28*
   a. *Why did the religious leaders question John's work of baptizing people out in the desert?*

- **How did they challenge his credentials?**

As the people's religious leaders, the Pharisees and others in the Jewish ruling council wanted control over all things religious in the life of the people. These leaders seemed mainly to have been concerned about John's credentials. First of all, they demanded, who gave him the right to baptize people? Normally in those days people baptized themselves. But John was baptizing people who came to him. The religious leaders were also likely concerned about John's call to *everyone* to repent in preparation for the Messiah. One could understand the need to baptize Gentiles (non-Jews) who accepted the God of Israel as the true God. But it was probably disturbing to the ruling council that John was baptizing Jews and calling even their leaders to repentance (Matt. 3:8-9).

If any group members raise questions about baptism, note that John's practice of baptism was different from the baptism that the church has practiced ever since Christ's death and resurrection. John's baptism had to do with preparation, showing repentance for sin (Matt. 3:11; Mark 1:4; Acts 19:1-6), while baptism in Christ symbolizes the washing away of sin and our dying to sin and coming to new life in him through the power of his death and resurrection (Rom. 6:3-10).

Recognize that some Christian traditions have differing views on baptism. If anyone has a strong opinion about his or her own view, offer to discuss the matter another time so that you can continue together with the material for this lesson. Whenever you discuss this topic with someone, it can be helpful to note that all who follow the Bible as their guide have closer positions on baptism than they might think. For example, churches that

c.   What testimony does John the Baptist give about Jesus in verses 32-34?

John states that he saw the Holy Spirit come down from heaven "as a dove" and remain on Jesus. (Though the gospel writer John does not specifically mention the baptism of Jesus, we can tell that's the context in which John the Baptist gives this testimony—see Matt. 3:16.) John the Baptist also says he would not have known Jesus except that God had revealed this to him before he baptized Jesus. In addition, John testifies here that Jesus is the Son of God.

Note: In a way John's comment about not knowing Jesus may seem strange to us, since we know the two are relatives (Luke 1:36). But the Bible gives no further details about their extended-family relationship. It's possible that they did not know each other well enough to recognize one another. This happens among relatives still today, especially if they have grown up in different regions, as John and Jesus did (see Luke 1:26, 39).

- **How was Jesus' identity revealed to John?**

John says, "The one who sent me to baptize with water told me . . ." (John 1:33). In other words, the Spirit of God had told John beforehand. As we learn from other gospel accounts, God spoke and identified Jesus as his Son during Jesus' baptism (Matt. 3:17; Mark 1:11; Luke 3:22). So the source of John's testimony is God alone.

- **How do you think the religious leaders would have responded to John's testimony?**

4.   *John 1:35-42*

   a.   Why do you think John the Baptist repeated this testimony to his disciples the next day?

- **Who were these disciples?**

John understood that the purpose of his own ministry was drawing to a close—or at least changing (see John 3:27-30). John likely wanted to emphasize Jesus' role as Messiah in order to direct his disciples to follow Jesus.

When they heard John's testimony about Jesus, two disciples who were with John went to follow Jesus (1:37). One is later identified as Andrew, and the other, who is not named, may well have been John the disciple. Many students of the Bible have suggested that this may be John the disciple because he would know the details of this event and he is not named elsewhere in this gospel as being called to discipleship.

b. What did these disciples do next?

- **Why do you think these disciples followed Jesus?**

When the two disciples began following Jesus, he encouraged them to come and see what he was all about. Before long, they were convinced that Jesus was the Messiah, so Andrew immediately went to tell his brother Simon and to bring him to Jesus. When Jesus met him, he gave Simon a new name, Peter, which means "rock" (see Matt. 16:18), and he followed Jesus as well.

You might note here that the disciple John had a brother, James, who also became one of Jesus' disciples. In the gospel account of Matthew we find Jesus calling Simon (Peter) and Andrew, and then a little while later he calls James and John to follow him (Matt. 4:18-22). Summarize briefly and encourage group members to read later all four gospel accounts of Jesus' calling his disciples (see also Mark 1:16-20; Luke 5:1-11). For your present discussion, you can simply note that while these stories have some different details, they combine important points from different perspectives to show that these believers heard God's call (through Jesus, through God's prophet John, and through their training in the Scriptures) and that they responded by following Jesus and bringing others to meet him.

Even at this early stage in Jesus' ministry, we can see how the message about him travels quickly through a web of connections. Nearly everyone has some interconnectedness with others, and news travels fast through this network of relationships.

- **Think of your own web of connections. If you had just met Jesus and were convinced he was the promised Messiah, whom would you tell first?**

5. *John 1:43-51*
   a. Describe the events of the following day. How did the web of connections expand?

Note that Jesus called Philip to be a disciple—in fact, the text implies that Jesus *searched him out and found him.* Then Philip, in turn, went and found his friend Nathanael to tell him about Jesus.

- **What was it about Jesus that caused these people to drop everything and follow him?**

As the introduction to this study explains, it was an honor in those days to be called to follow a great teacher (rabbi) and become his disciple. It was an even greater honor to be called by a teacher who was showing signs of being the Messiah, as witnessed and recommended by John the Baptist.

For any young man in the Jewish community this would have been the opportunity of a lifetime. So, as the Bible tells us, they dropped everything and followed Jesus.

b.   *What do we learn about Jesus and Nathanael in verses 47-51?*

As soon as Nathanael heard Philip say that the Messiah was from Nazareth, he was taken aback and said, "Can anything good come from there?"

- **Why do you think Nathanael had such a low opinion of Nazareth?**

Nathanael's comment may have meant that Nazareth was a rival to his own hometown (Cana—see John 21:2), but from his point of view Nazareth may simply have had a bad reputation or been an undesirable place to live.

- **Have you ever heard people talk this way about certain cities or regions? How accurate or fair are such statements?**

Jesus took Nathanael by surprise, however, when they eventually met. Jesus said Nathanael was "a true Israelite, in whom there [was] nothing false." Nathanael might well have thought this way about himself, but this comment apparently raised his curiosity. "How do you know me?" he asked (John 1:48). Jesus then made clear that a person from Nazareth could be quite remarkable: he said he'd seen Nathanael "still under the fig tree" before Philip had called on him. In other words, Jesus was able to tell Nathanael what he'd been doing even before Nathanael had heard of Jesus. (See also John 2:24-25.)

c.   *How did Nathanael react to Jesus' comments?*

Nathanael was fully convinced that Jesus was the Messiah, as Philip had said. Nathanael was not simply amazed; he responded with a comprehensive statement: "Rabbi, you are the Son of God; you are the King of Israel."

- **What do these titles indicate?**

Nathanael's response indicated that he knew Jesus was not the usual rabbi but the Son of God, the messianic King of Israel—the promised deliverer the people had been longing for.

d.   What assurances did Jesus then give to Nathanael?

Jesus replied with a promise that recalled an ancient promise God had made to Jacob (Israel), the father of the Israelites. In Genesis 28:10-17 we read of a vision Jacob had, in which angels were going up and down a stairway that led to heaven. In that vision God had promised to give Jacob many descendants and to bless all the peoples of the earth through him. Jesus was now saying that he was that stairway or gateway to heaven and that he would be the one to bring God's blessing to all people. We'll find Jesus making similar statements as we study more of the book of John (see John 3:16-17; 10:9; 14:6).

Question for Reflection

Compare and contrast the way the early followers of Jesus responded to him. How do you respond to him? How do you share that response with others?

Invite group members to talk about their own responses to Jesus by sharing one or two examples of their experiences with him. As leader, be prepared to set the tone for discussion by sharing some of your own experiences. Note together that sharing this way in your group setting can be good practice for sharing about Jesus with other people in our lives.

Lesson 3
John 2

Of Weddings and Worship

Additional Related Scriptures

Genesis 49:10-12

Exodus 12

Psalm 69:9

Isaiah 56:7

Matthew 21:12-17

Mark 11:17

Luke 8:10

John 1:51; 4:23-34; 10:9; 14:6

Hebrews 10:1-18

Introductory Notes

In the Bible the kingdom of heaven is often described as a great feast and celebration. Jesus himself describes it as a wedding banquet in one of his parables (Matt. 22:1-14). In the book of Revelation, also written by Jesus' disciple John, the great celebration in heaven is called "the wedding supper of the Lamb" (Rev. 19:7, 9). So as we learn more about Jesus in the gospel of John, we can see that it would be natural for him to enjoy celebrating with others. In addition, it's not surprising that in John 2 we find Jesus attending a wedding party and that this event becomes the setting for his first miracle.

In the second part of this lesson, as we look at the rest of John 2, we observe another side of Jesus. He enters the temple in Jerusalem and clears it of people who turned a worship area into an oppressive marketplace. In this important episode we see how Jesus comes to replace the temple and its system of sacrifices with himself, changing the worship of God to take place through him alone (John 2:21; see 1:51; 4:23-34; 10:9; 14:6).

Optional Share Question

Describe a fun wedding that you attended. What made it fun?

1. *John 2:1-5*

   a. *What problem developed at the wedding Jesus attended?*

   • **How might the bride and groom and their families have felt about this?**

A wedding feast in ancient Palestine could go on for a week, and the bridegroom was expected to keep all guests fully supplied with food and drink. So it was a serious breach of hospitality to have the wine supply depleted before the celebration ended. The bridegroom's reputation as a host would be ruined. This crisis likely would have created a sense of panic on the part of the bride and groom as well as their families.

b. *Describe the conversation between Jesus and his mother. What do we learn about Mary from her response? What do we learn about Jesus?*

In her heart, Mary knew Jesus could do something about this potentially ruinous event. It's difficult, though, to know precisely what her intent was when she said to Jesus, "They have no more wine."

- **Why does Jesus seem to distance himself from his mother?**

Jesus' reply appears to be curt and formal. Yet he is simply pointing out that his role as Messiah could not be prompted by human demand. God, not Mary, would determine when the time to reveal his glory had come.

It may be helpful to point out that this conversation between Mary and Jesus is linguistically polite and cordial. Mary makes a simple statement, and Jesus simply makes clear that his heavenly Father and not his earthly mother is the governor of his life and calling.

- **Does Mary understand what Jesus is saying to her?**

From the text it appears that Mary understands, because her statement to the servants, "Do whatever he tells you," shows that she trusts he will do whatever is right. Not only is this first miracle a revelation of Jesus' power; it also reveals Mary's faith in him.

If any group members are from a Roman Catholic background, be sensitive to the fact that they may revere Mary more highly than most other believers do. For example, someone might suggest that Mary knew better than Jesus, or that Jesus was afraid and that she knew he could perform a miracle here. Without arguing points of doctrine, simply suggest other possibilities and guide the discussion so that Jesus is honored as God. Being exposed to clear, biblical teaching over time will help members of the group alter long-held views that may come from sources other than the Bible.

2. *John 2:6-10*

a. *What did Jesus do next? Describe the results.*

Jesus told the servants to fill with water six jars that were normally used for ceremonial washing. Then he told them to draw some out and take it to the master of the banquet. (This person was like a master of ceremonies hired by the groom to direct the wedding festivities.)

- **How did the master of the banquet respond?**

He was surprised at the quality of this wine, so he complimented the bridegroom for saving the best wine till last.

b. *What was the crucial result for the wedding celebration?*

The new abundance of wine and its higher quality saved the bridegroom's reputation and ensured that the feast could continue.

c. *What does this miracle tell us about the depth of Jesus' care for people?*

This miracle was an amazing sign of God's gracious love in Jesus, showing that even the reputation of a bridegroom from the small town of Cana can be important to God. God cares about all our needs, and when we have eyes of faith to see this, we are often amazed at God's attention to the details of our lives—not to mention that we often receive more than is needed. Just as Jesus provided the wedding party with premium wine, the Lord often provides us with high-quality abundance so that we can celebrate and share God's goodness with others.

Recent commentators also see a connection between the water of baptism being replaced by the wine of God's kingdom. In other words, this miracle can be seen to reveal Jesus as the one who came to replace the constant need for repentance and cleansing with the overabundant joy and celebration of God's everlasting kingdom (see Gen. 49:10-12).

Note: Some group members may wonder if this miracle implies, as some have claimed, that Jesus condoned drunkenness. If so, remind people that Jesus himself said he came to fulfill God's law, not to abolish it (Matt. 5:17-20). This means he came to show people how to live God's way—the way of true righteousness. In the Bible, drunkenness is always portrayed as foolishness, which goes against God's way of wisdom and righteousness (see Prov. 20:1; 23:19-21; 26:9; Isa. 19:14; 24:20; Luke 12:45-46; Eph. 5:18). On the other hand, the Bible also portrays wine and feasting as signs of celebration in the kingdom of God (Isa. 25:6; 55:1-2; 62:8-9; Matt. 22:1-14; Luke 22:20). So while drunkenness is foolish and wrong, a responsible use of fermented drinks can be appropriate for celebrating God's goodness and blessing. (Some historians have suggested that the wine used in those days was diluted or not fermented, but the Bible offers plenty of evidence to show that misuse of wine often caused drunkenness.) If any group members have a particular sensitivity to this topic—for example, because of alcohol abuse in their family—be sure to show kindness and compassion while also pointing out the bigger picture of God's lavish care for us—including the responsible enjoyment of God's good gifts.

3. John 2:11
What did this miracle ultimately accomplish?

John's summary here is an important teaching tool about the twofold purpose of miracles. Jesus' miracle at Cana revealed his glory as the Son of God (Messiah) and strengthened the faith of his disciples.

- **How do you think you'd have responded to this miracle if you were one of Jesus' disciples?**

This question gives you as leader an opportunity to gauge the understanding of the group. Encourage group members to think about the impact such a miracle might make on them. It's interesting that Jesus would choose to do this miracle first. And it appears from the story that only Jesus, Mary, the servants, and the disciples knew about it. Mention to your group that you'll encounter several more miracles in Jesus' teaching ministry as you study the book of John. It will be interesting to see the differences between these miracles and discover what they teach us about Jesus.

4. John 2:12-16
a. *Who went with Jesus to Capernaum after the wedding celebration? Why do you think they went along?*

The community of Capernaum became a sort of headquarters for Jesus in his teaching ministry (Matt. 4:13). So it's interesting that Jesus' mother and brothers accompanied him and his disciples there after the wedding instead of going back to their hometown, Nazareth, which was in the opposite direction. Perhaps they went with Jesus to Capernaum so they could go together to the upcoming Passover feast in Jerusalem. Capernaum was located on one of the major routes from Galilee to Jerusalem, while Nazareth was more remote.

You might also note that the entire area Jesus covered in his teaching ministry was about 60 miles (96 km) by 120 miles (193 km), with most of his activity within 20 miles (32 km) of Capernaum (see the map in the study guide). In the book of John we'll see Jesus crisscross this area several times.

If questions arise about Jesus' brothers, it may be helpful to know that some churches say they were half-brothers of Jesus by a different mother or that the word "brothers" in John 2:12 means "cousins" or "companions." If anyone in your group holds to these or other views (usually in connection with special reverence for Mary), simply acknowledge what the passage says and indicate that other passages also mention Jesus' brothers (Matt. 12:46-47; 13:55; John 7:1-10; Act 1:14; Gal. 1:19).

b. Where did Jesus go next, and why?

Jesus went to Jerusalem to celebrate the Passover, one of the main holy feasts of Judaism.

- **What was the significance of the Passover?**

Again point group members to the glossary. The Passover celebration recalled the time when the Israelites (now known as the Jews) were freed after more than four hundred years of slavery in Egypt (Ex. 12). The Israelites' children were spared one night when God *passed over* their homes and did not allow a plague of death to enter there because the people had spread the blood of a sacrificed lamb on their doorframes. On that same night, however, all the firstborn sons of other families in Egypt died. This was the final plague that God sent to punish the Egyptians during the time of Moses. It was so devastating that the king of Egypt (pharaoh) finally agreed to free God's people Israel. The Passover remembrance occurred each year in spring, and all Jewish men were required to go to the temple in Jerusalem for the celebration and ritual sacrifices.

c. Describe the scene in the temple. How did Jesus react to what he saw?

The temple built by Solomon had been destroyed. In about 20 B.C., Herod the Great, who ruled under Rome's authority, had begun rebuilding the temple on a grand scale, but it was not yet finished. The temple area had several courtyards designated as prayer areas for Jews and Gentiles. The court of the Gentiles was at the extreme outer portion, while the courts of men and women (reserved for Jews) were closer to the inner court, where the altars of sacrifice, the Holy Place, and the Most Holy Place were located.

During Passover it was necessary to have animals (cattle, sheep, and doves) available so that travelers could buy and offer them as sacrifices. It was also necessary for money changers to help travelers exchange their cash for currency acceptable by the temple authorities. For many years the animal vendors and money changers had set up their tables and vending booths outside the temple area. But in recent years the temple authorities had permitted them to move into the temple area in the large court designated for the Gentiles.

- **What action did Jesus take?**

Jesus was deeply disturbed at this turn of events, "so he made a whip of cords" and forcefully drove out the money changers and the animal vendors. In this way he "cleansed" the temple area of these intrusive elements.

- Why did Jesus respond so forcefully?

It's important to recognize that Jesus did not simply lose his temper because the temple had become a noisy marketplace. The court of the Gentiles was to be a place of prayer for non-Jews so that they could worship the one true God (Matt. 21:13; see Isa. 56:7). But the temple authorities who allowed vendors to take over this area did not care that non-Jews were unable to worship. In addition, the money changers and vendors appeared to be taking advantage of travelers by overcharging for goods and services while also robbing the temple of its role as a holy place (see Mark 11:17 and related text notes in the *NIV Study Bible*). Jesus was rightfully angry at this lack of concern and disrespect for others as well as for God.

In addition, as we can see from Jesus' later comment about his body as the temple (John 2:21), this episode points to his replacement of the temple and its system of sacrifices with himself; his mission as Messiah called for the sacrifice of his own life for our sin, once and for all (see Heb. 10:1-18).

Note: Some people have raised concerns about the timing of this episode in the book of John. John states that it occurs at the beginning of Jesus' ministry, and the other gospel accounts (Matthew, Mark, and Luke) mention a similar event near the end of Christ's ministry. It's probably not necessary to get into a discussion of whether the Bible is accurate, since we know its main purpose is to deliver the message of God's love rather than to provide a sequential history. But if group members are interested, you may wish to point out the following observations: If this is the same cleansing as recorded in the other gospel accounts, John may simply be placing it early in the narrative for thematic emphasis. John's account does tend to be more thematically constructed than the other gospel accounts. On the other hand, there are several differences between this account and the cleansing accounts in Matthew 21, Mark 11, and Luke 19. So this event might well have occurred during a different Passover feast. Such a cleansing could have occurred more than once during the three years of Jesus' teaching ministry.

5. *John 2:17-22*

    a. *What was the reaction of the disciples and the religious leaders after Jesus cleared the temple?*

The disciples remembered that the Scriptures had said, "Zeal for your house will consume me" (see Ps. 69:9).

- **What's the significance of this statement?**

John indicates here that Jesus cleansed the temple because he was zealous to promote and maintain God's honor. In other words, the disciples could understand that Jesus had compelling reasons for what he did.

The religious leaders, on the other hand, wanted to know what right Jesus had to clear out the vendors and money changers. They asked Jesus to produce a miraculous sign that would prove he had the authority to do this. But when Jesus replied with a veiled reference to his own death and resurrection ("Destroy this temple, and I will raise it again in three days"), they only became more confused and upset.

b.   What misunderstanding developed about the temple being destroyed?

The religious leaders assumed that Jesus was claiming he could rebuild the great temple in Jerusalem in just three days. So far it had taken forty-six years. They did not understand that he was speaking figuratively; in fact, they thought his claim was preposterous.

Note: You might explain here that Jesus often used allegories and "hidden sayings" when he responded to the unbelieving Jewish leaders. One day Jesus explained this approach to his disciples, saying, "The knowledge of the secrets of the kingdom of God has been given to you, but to others I speak in parables, so that, 'though seeing, they may not see, though hearing, they may not understand'" (Luke 8:10; see Matt. 13:35). A text note to Luke 8:10 in the *NIV Study Bible* adds, "This . . . does not express a desire that some would not understand, but simply states the sad truth that those who are not willing to receive Jesus' message will find the truth hidden from them."

- **When and how was the misunderstanding cleared up?**

John clarifies that "the temple [Jesus] had spoken of was his body. After he was raised from the dead, his disciples recalled what he had said" (John 2:21-22). What the temple and its sacrifices symbolized was embodied in Jesus' life and teaching. He embodied the sacrifices, he revealed the Father, and he was the dwelling place of God on earth. Jesus' response to the religious leaders could only be understood after his death and resurrection. For our sake he died on a cross and was buried, and on the third day God raised his body to life again (John 20:1-9; Acts 10:40; 1 Cor. 15:4). Only after he completed his mission did it become clear that he fulfilled the purpose of the Old Testament temple and its sacrifices and became the one way to God and to life in God's kingdom forever (see John 1:51; 4:23-34; 10:9; 14:6; Heb. 10:1-18).

6. *John 2:23-25*

   a.   How did the crowds in Jerusalem react to Jesus?

Many people saw the miraculous signs Jesus did, and they believed in him. As we learn from later episodes in Jesus' ministry, however, although people believed in him because of the miracles they saw, many had no trusting faith in Jesus as the messianic redeemer. When he presented teachings that they didn't expect from the Messiah, many followers turned away (John 6:60-69).

   b.   What was Jesus' reaction to the people's praise?

- **Did Jesus need their praise?**

Jesus knew that the people's faith was shallow and insincere. The same word for "belief" in verse 23 is used again in verse 24 to say that Jesus did not "entrust" himself to them. He knew how selfish, weak, and unreliable people were. He knew their faith was not deep and that they lacked solid commitment. That's why he came to offer salvation, to shed his blood as a sacrifice so that death would "pass over" them, to set them free from their slavery to sin.

Question for Reflection

   What new things have you learned about Jesus in this lesson? Reflect on the events you've studied here, noting whom Jesus helped and whom he rebuked.

Lesson 4
John 3

The Gospel in a Nutshell

Additional Related Scriptures

Numbers 21:4-9
Ezekiel 36:25-26
Matthew 14:1-12
Mark 6:14-29

John 2:25; 19:38-42
2 Thessalonians 2:10
2 Peter 3:9

Introductory Notes

John 3:16, a central passage in this lesson, is sometimes described as the gospel in a nutshell. It clearly and briefly explains why Jesus came to earth, how we should respond to him, and what the ultimate result will be.

Unfortunately this verse has often been trivialized—for example, when people post only the chapter and verse number on billboards or hold them high on banners at sporting events. Many others who see only "John 3:16" expressed this way do not understand the tremendous importance of the words behind this Scripture reference.

Whether you are reading John 3:16 and the verses around it for the first time or the fiftieth time, pray for understanding and insight into its meaning within the episode John describes here. Ask for the wisdom you'll need when you share the message of John 3:16 with someone who needs to understand.

Jesus spoke these words to Nicodemus, who came to ask about Jesus' mission. Though Nicodemus showed some skepticism at first and was confused by some of the word pictures Jesus used, he kept asking for understanding. And Jesus replied with these words—among others—that have become so well known today: "God so loved the world that he gave his one and only Son, that whoever believes in him shall not perish but have eternal life" (John 3:16).

Optional Share Question

Describe a time when you were scared (or at least a bit nervous) to talk with someone about something you did not understand. How might that experience help you listen to others and encourage them to talk about things they don't understand?

1. *John 3:1-4*

   a. Who was Nicodemus, and why do you think he came at night to visit Jesus?

   John indicates that Nicodemus was a teacher of the Jews and a member of the Jewish ruling council (also known as the Sanhedrin; see glossary). Rome delegated a great deal of authority to this body for governing the day-to-day affairs of the Jewish people. The only thing the council could not do without Rome's judgment was to sentence a person to death.

   Some interpreters have said Nicodemus came at night because he did not want the other Jewish leaders to know he was visiting Jesus. This may well have been the case, since the religious leaders had already shown lots of skepticism about Jesus. Other Bible scholars, however, suggest that John might have used the phrase "at night" to show that Nicodemus was figuratively living in the dark. In support of their idea, they note Jesus' later comments about people loving "darkness instead of light" (John 3:19).

   - **Do you think Nicodemus was already a firm believer in Jesus? Explain.**

   While discussing Nicodemus's character, note with your group that these verses immediately follow John 2:24-25, which say Jesus did not entrust himself to people and did not need their testimony because he knew what was in them. In other words, reflect together on whether the account of Nicodemus's visit is thematically linked to the previous paragraph in John's gospel. It's interesting, at least, that Nicodemus cites Jesus' miracles as the main reason for believing in him (see John 2:23; 3:2). (If necessary, remind the group that chapters and verse numbers were not originally part of the biblical text. Chapter divisions were introduced in A.D. 1205, and verse designations were first published in 1565 for the New Testament and 1571 for the Old Testament.)

   You might also mention that after Jesus died, Nicodemus helped Joseph, a secret disciple who was also a member of the ruling council (Mark 15:43), to remove Jesus' body from the cross and place it in a tomb. So apparently Nicodemus grew in his faith toward Jesus and also became a secret disciple by the time of Jesus' death (see John 19:38-42).

   b. What did Nicodemus say to Jesus, and how did Jesus respond?

   Nicodemus addressed Jesus as "Rabbi," a term of respect that means "teacher." He stated that since Jesus was able to perform miracles, he must have been sent by God.

   Jesus then immediately zeroed in on a personal need he saw in Nicodemus. Though he spoke indirectly, as he often did with religious leaders, Jesus implied that Nicodemus had to be reborn by the power of the Holy Spirit.

You might point out that this is the first place in the book of John where Jesus uses the phrase, "I tell you the truth" (John 3:3). A more literal translation of the Greek text here reads, "Truly, truly." Jesus often uses this phrase for special emphasis. In other words, Jesus was saying, "Listen closely because this is important!" Jesus was indicating that Nicodemus needed a radical change of heart. Though he was a highly educated teacher, Nicodemus had to start over again by being spiritually reborn.

    c.   Why was Nicodemus confused by what Jesus said?

- **What would a religious leader like Nicodemus tend to assume about his own standing before God?**

As a ruler of the Jews and a Pharisee in good standing, Nicodemus would have learned from his religious tradition that he could be sure of a place in God's kingdom. Jesus was saying, however, that all people, even a ruler and teacher like Nicodemus, had to be "born again" or "born from above" (NRSV). In other words, a religious leader's standing among the Jews and his obedience to the law did not guarantee entrance into heaven. This information would have totally confused Nicodemus because it conflicted with much of what he'd been taught in Judaism.

- **What does Nicodemus's response tell us about him?**

The tone of Nicodemus's response in John 3:4 sounds similar to that of other responses we've heard from religious leaders in our study so far (see 1:21-25; 2:18-20). It sounds as if he thought Jesus was saying something preposterous.

We can't be sure whether Nicodemus was using a debate tactic here or if he was genuinely curious about the process of being born again, but we can be sure that Jesus was looking straight into this man's heart. Even if Nicodemus was trying to avoid a personal conversation and attempting to get the discussion back to a theoretical level, Jesus knew what Nicodemus needed to hear.

2. John 3:5-9

    a.   How does Jesus explain the concept of being "born again?"

Jesus explains that this rebirth is spiritual rather than physical.

- **How do people use the phrase "born again" today?**

- **Is this different from the way Jesus used it? Is it the same? Explain.**

When a person is born again, God's Spirit changes that person on the inside, and this shows by the effects it causes in a person's way of life. Jesus uses the example of the wind to illustrate this point. We cannot really see it, but we can see its results.

- **What do the terms "water and the Spirit" represent?**

These terms tie in with repentance and new life. A helpful cross reference is Ezekiel 36:25-26, where God says to his people, "I will sprinkle clean water on you, and you will be clean. . . . I will give you a new heart and put a new spirit in you." In the Old Testament water was used for ceremonial washing and purification.

These terms also sound like an early reference to Christian baptism. John the Baptist used water for a baptism that symbolized repentance, and he said that the Messiah (Jesus) would baptize with the Holy Spirit (John 1:33). After the Holy Spirit came on Pentecost, Jesus' disciples also baptized new believers, who were promised "the gift of the Holy Spirit" (Acts 2:38).

From the context of his conversation with Nicodemus, it seems clear that Jesus was calling Nicodemus to repentance and faith.

- **How does Jesus' response show concern and compassion for Nicodemus?**

Jesus is clearly taking the time to explain more to Nicodemus about entering the kingdom of God. He's also showing that a religious ruler who wants to listen is welcome to do so. Though Jesus sometimes spoke harshly to religious leaders and others who had closed their hearts to him (see Matt. 23), he is showing Nicodemus that he loves even a Pharisee who might argue with him. As Romans 5:8, 10 reminds us, "God demonstrates his own love for us in this: While we were still sinners, Christ died for us. . . . When we were God's enemies, we were reconciled to him through the death of his Son."

b. *How does Nicodemus react to Jesus' explanation?*

- **How is this response different from his previous response to Jesus?**

Nicodemus may be skeptical, but he appears to be softening to the amazing mystery of Jesus' words. Note that he doesn't argue but simply asks, "How can this be?"

Remind group members that Jesus was suggesting something quite revolutionary to Nicodemus. He was saying that a person like Nicodemus was unfit for entrance into heaven unless he repented and was spiritually reborn by the power of God's Spirit. Again, this would have been a highly disturbing idea to a ruler of the Jews. And yet Nicodemus asks for more information rather than shutting Jesus out.

3. *John 3:10-15*

   a. *How does Jesus respond to this statement by Nicodemus?*

   - **Is Jesus chiding Nicodemus? Challenging him? Encouraging him?**

Jesus points out that because Nicodemus is a teacher in Israel he should know the basics. Jesus then says that if Nicodemus does not understand earthly concepts, how can he understand heavenly things? Next Jesus indicates that he, as the Son of Man, surely knows how a person can enter the kingdom of God (heaven). He has this information because he is from heaven and he knows the will of the Father. He came from heaven to provide a way for believers to enter heaven.

   b. *What does the event mentioned in verse 14 have to do with Jesus? (See Num. 21:4-9.)*

   - **Why do you think Jesus includes this Old Testament example?**

Numbers 21:4-9 tells of a punishment God sent the Israelites when they were complaining in the wilderness after being freed from slavery in Egypt. God punished them by sending venomous snakes among them. The people soon repented of their sinful complaints and asked Moses to plead with God for deliverance. God told Moses to make a bronze snake and set it up on a pole, and whoever looked at this snake would be spared from death.

Jesus was saying that just as Moses lifted up the serpent in the wilderness, the Son of Man (a messianic term Jesus often used to describe himself) had to be lifted up to provide deliverance for all who looked to him. This comment may have been confusing to Nicodemus, but since we know the rest of the story, we can tell that Jesus was talking about being lifted up and dying on the cross so that all who looked to him and believed in him would be saved from death and have eternal life. It took faith on the part of the ancient Israelites to look at the bronze serpent and be saved. By using this example, Jesus was saying it takes faith on the part of all who look to him to be saved as well. His death would cover the punishment of death for their sins.

4. *John 3:16-21*

   a. What does John 3:16 mean to you?

Invite group members to share personal responses. Some may have a story they'd like to tell about sharing this verse and its meaning with someone. Others may wish to share some thoughts on their own personal belief in Jesus as Savior.

This statement contains the essence of the gospel (good news) message. It describes God's gracious love for humanity and God's plan to save people through the sacrifice of his Son, the promised Messiah. Note too that this statement refers to the whole world. Jesus' life is more than valuable enough to pay for the sins of all people—not just believing Jews but believing Gentiles as well. In addition, because his death destroys the power of sin, Jesus' finished work has the power to free God's creation (the whole universe) from the effects of sin (see Gen. 3:17-19; Rom. 8:20-25; Rev. 1:1-4).

   b. What happens to people who do not believe this good news?

Jesus says they are condemned already because they are living in the darkness of sin and refuse to come out into the light of righteousness.

   • **Why do people love the darkness? Why do they wish to remain in the darkness?**

The emphasis here is on the choice of unbelievers to remain disconnected from God. It's not a matter of God's judgment prohibiting them from being saved; it's simply a matter of rejecting Jesus and remaining in a state of unbelief.

   c. Why do they choose not to believe?

According to verses 19-20, unbelievers do not wish to have their sinful deeds exposed in the light.

   • **What does light do?**

One quality of light is to show imperfection. A person who trusts in the saving work of Jesus has to be willing to admit being imperfect—that is, being sinful and in need of God's forgiveness.

Light also reveals the truth about something. A person who "lives by the truth" (John 3:21) faces up to his or her need for repentance and faith in Jesus, and the light shows that the person has done this through the power of God. In Jesus, God has expressed his love for the world, so now people have to respond to that love—and they do that through the work of God in their lives, or they refuse to believe and thus remain in the darkness.

5. John 3:22-30

a.   *When Jesus and his disciples go out into the countryside, what controversy develops?*

- **What do you think John's disciples are concerned about?**

There is controversy over the baptisms that John as well as Jesus are doing. Again it seems that the Jewish religious leaders are behind this dispute, since it has to do with "ceremonial washing" (3:25). This seems to lead John's disciples to question why Jesus is becoming more popular. They might even see Jesus' ministry as competing with John's.

b.   *How does John the Baptist deal with this controversy?*

- **How does John compare himself to Jesus?**

Once again John teaches his followers that he is less important than Jesus is. John uses the example of being like the bridegroom's attendant (best man) at a wedding. Just as it would be inappropriate for the best man at a wedding to get more attention than the groom, it would be outside of John's role as the Lord's prophet to get more attention than the Messiah.

John recognizes that his role will soon come to an end. In fact, this passage tells us John will be put in prison (3:24). (From Matthew 14:1-12 and Mark 6:14-29 we learn that John the Baptist is later imprisoned and executed by Herod, the ruler of Galilee, for preaching against Herod's unlawful marriage to his brother's wife, Herodias.)

John indicates, however, that he looks forward to the Messiah's taking over. John's joy is now complete because he has fulfilled his work as a forerunner. He also acknowledges that the Messiah must now become greater while John himself becomes less. He is the last of the prophets called to tell of the coming Messiah, and now the Messiah is here.

6. John 3:31-36

Notice that these verses repeat much of the content of John 3:11-18. Why do you think this information is repeated?

In verses 31-36 the gospel writer John gives a summary of the main teaching in the preceding episodes of Jesus' ministry. Perhaps because the explanation by Jesus in 3:11-18 is so important for understanding the gospel message, the writer repeats its main points before moving on to another section of his gospel account. (Note that the NIV treats these verses as if they are spoken by John the Baptist, but other versions treat them as a narrative summary—see, for example, the NRSV, RSV, and TEV. If necessary, remind group members that quotation marks and other punctuation are added by translators; the original Greek text has no punctuation.)

- **How would you describe, in summary, the main teachings of this section?**

Invite group members to give their own summaries, thinking especially of how they would explain this section of Scripture to someone who wanted to know about Jesus and the gospel message.

Question for Reflection

If you had been Nicodemus, how do you think you might have responded to Jesus' words?

Lesson 5
John 4:1-42

A Surprising Encounter

Additional Related Scriptures

Genesis 33:19

Joshua 8:33; 24:32

2 Kings 17

Ezra 4

Luke 6:46-49

1 Corinthians 10:31

James 1:22-27

Introductory Notes

In this lesson we discover Jesus teaching a Samaritan woman about salvation. It's probably no accident that John the gospel writer includes this story shortly after the story of Nicodemus and his visit with Jesus. Even a brief comparison reveals two very different individuals. Not only was one a man and the other a woman, but Nicodemus and the Samaritan woman were also different nationally, morally, and socially. Nicodemus was a community leader, while the woman was likely an outcast—and yet they had one thing in common. They both needed what only Jesus could offer.

This lesson reminds us that we all need to come to Christ with empty hands. However we see ourselves, we can trust that only Christ can offer us what we really need.

Optional Share Question

When you were growing up, how could you tell who was part of the "in" crowd? How were people on the outside treated?

1. *John 4:1-3*

   What prompted Jesus to leave Judea?

The religious leaders were becoming more aware of Jesus as his ministry increased and John the Baptist's ministry decreased. As a result, the Pharisees' opposition would soon shift toward Jesus.

- **Why would Jesus go to Galilee?**

The religious leaders would be more likely to be in Judea. In Galilee, Jesus would be able to conduct his ministry without their constant scrutiny.

2. John 4:4-6

a. Why would Jesus have to go through Samaria?

- **What was unusual about taking this route?**

In some ways this question might seem unnecessary. A quick look at a map of Jesus' ministry (like the one in the study guide) shows that the most direct route from Judea to Galilee was through Samaria. But most Jews in those days wouldn't take that route, because the Jews and Samaritans despised one another (see John 4:9).

The problem was rooted in long-standing religious differences. Back in 722 B.C. when the Assyrians captured Samaria, they deported many Israelite leaders and replaced them with people from Assyria and neighboring countries. As a result, the worship of God in the region of Samaria became mixed with the religions of other peoples, at least for a time (see 2 Kings 17). The Samaritans, however, insisted that they were the true worshipers of God and that the Jews were heretics who had rejected the holy place of worship on Mount Gerizim established by their ancestors (see Josh. 8:33; John 4:19-20). Later, after the people of Judah were exiled to Babylon and were set free to return and rebuild Jerusalem, tensions resurfaced. At first some of the Samaritan leaders offered to help rebuild the temple in Jerusalem, but the Jewish leaders refused. As a result, corrupt leaders in Samaria tried to have the rebuilding stopped (see Ezra 4). All this led to further hostility that continued for hundreds of years and was still festering in Jesus' day.

Because of this hostility, most Jews would cross the Jordan River and travel along the east bank to avoid going through Samaria. But Jesus decided to take the road that ran through Samaria.

- **Reflect on the meaning of "had to go" in verse 4.**

The phrase "had to go" may actually indicate a sense of mission and an opportunity for Jesus to teach his disciples. Just as John 3 noted that God loved not only the Jewish people but also the Gentiles, John 4 provides an illustration in which Jesus brings the good news to Samaria, which the Jews saw as a land of Gentiles.

b. Describe where Jesus went and how he felt.

Note again John's attention to location. Jesus went to a place in Samaria called Sychar. This town was near a historic place—a plot of ground with a well that the Old Testament patriarch Jacob "had given to his son Joseph" (John 4:12; see Gen. 33:19; Josh. 24:32).

- **What details in these verses show us that Jesus was human?**

We sometimes forget that Jesus was subject to the limitations of a human body. Like everyone else, Jesus had to walk hot, dusty roads to go from place to place. This passage indicates that he was hot and tired. By the time Jesus sat down to rest by Jacob's well, it was the hottest time of day—around noon, "the sixth hour" after sunrise.

3. *John 4:7-9*

   What does Jesus ask of the Samaritan woman, and how does she respond?

The woman is obviously surprised that Jesus is speaking to her and asking her for a drink of water. In the culture of that day it would be highly unusual for a man to speak to a woman he did not know.

- **What does her reply tell us about the relationship between Jews and Samaritans?**

As explained earlier, Jews and Samaritans would not normally have contact with each other. Jesus, however, was not prejudiced or concerned with social conventions. He was concerned about saving people from sin. So when he met this woman, he started up a conversation with her that would change her life.

4. *John 4:10-15*

   a. *What does Jesus say that arouses the woman's curiosity?*

- **Does he answer her question?**

Jesus doesn't answer the woman's question directly, but he says he can give her something called "living water." He also says that if only she knew who he was, she would ask him for this water.

- **What do her responses in verses 11-12 show us?**

- **Does she really understand him?**

It seems clear that she is trying to figure out who this man is. "Are you greater than our father Jacob, who gave us the well?" she asks. But she is also trying to understand Jesus literally. She sees that he doesn't even have a pail—how could he offer her water?

b. What is Jesus really offering the woman?

- **What does the imagery of water suggest about the life Jesus offers?**

In a desert climate the availability of water means the difference between life and death. Jesus tells the Samaritan woman that he can give her a kind of water that will quench her thirst forever. He offers her "living water" that will quench her spiritual thirst, and he describes it as a spring that wells up to provide eternal life.

c. What does the woman's request in verse 15 tell us about her?

- **What does she think Jesus is saying?**

The Samaritan woman senses that Jesus is offering her something important, and she wants it. But she still seems to be thinking only about her physical thirst. How wonderful it would be to have water that quenched her thirst so fully that she wouldn't have to keep coming back to the local well!

Scholars note that this woman probably was drawing water at noontime because she was somewhat of a social outcast. The menial work of drawing water was usually done by women in the cool hours of the day. But this woman, who had had five husbands (John 4:18), probably came at this time to avoid disapproving stares and comments from others in the community.

5. *John 4:16-18*

a. *Why do you think Jesus tells the woman to call her husband and come back?*

- **What is his purpose in bringing up her marital status?**

- **What does he want to get across to her?**

Jesus knows that in order to help this person, he needs to take their discussion out of the abstract (from the topic of living water) and into the concrete (about things going on in her everyday life). Because Jesus is not only human but also God, he knows all about this woman's life. He knows how many husbands she has had, and, more important, how desperately she is searching for happiness and fulfillment in life. By saying "Go, call your husband," Jesus is calling her to face a matter of struggle and failure in her life, and by saying "come back," he is calling her to come to God and be satisfied. In effect, Jesus is calling this woman to repentance. *Repent* literally means "turn around" or "turn back." Jesus is inviting her to give up her old ways and come back to God, the only one who can truly satisfy all her needs.

   b.   *How does she try to sidestep Jesus' invitation?*

   •   **Do you think she is feeling guilty? Explain.**

It's interesting that the woman does not technically tell a lie, but she does shade the truth by leaving out important details. Jesus' request may well have made her feel guilty. And her response is vague enough to be useful in stalling or changing the subject of conversation. It may be that she has told this half-truth on other occasions. Though we don't know the details about her marriages, it seems clear that this woman faced some moral struggles in her life and needed to make some changes. When Jesus reveals what he knows about her past and her present situation, we can see that she's been hiding something—and it turns out to be information that would be socially embarrassing for most people. His knowledge about her private life must have been unnerving to her.

   •   **Does it ever bother you that God knows all the details of your private life? Why or why not?**

6.   *John 4:19-26*
   a.   *What subject does the Samaritan woman take up next?*

   •   **Why do you think she does this?**

When things get uncomfortable on a personal level, changing the subject is a natural defense. The Samaritan woman switches subjects to talk about theological things. It's interesting that she switches from moral issues in her personal life to worship-related issues in the lives of Jews and Samaritans. While admitting that Jesus is right about her personal life ("I can see that you are a prophet"), she charges into a debate about worship wars that have been going on for centuries, and she makes clear that she believes the Jews are wrong to worship in Jerusalem. But she doesn't realize that Jesus knows what she really needs.

   •   **What does the Samaritan woman really need?**

The Samaritan woman needs a renewed relationship with God. She needs to face her own unfaithfulness to God, and she needs Jesus to reveal that truth so that she can be restored and live God's way. There is pain involved, but Jesus knows this pain is necessary.

- **Why do we sometimes prefer discussions on a theological rather than a personal level?**

It's often easier to discuss matters of the head (ideas, theology, philosophy, history) rather than matters of the heart (personal feelings, emotions, relationships, failures). Heart change is also personally difficult.

- **What does Jesus teach the woman about worship?**

Jesus uses this change of discussion as a teaching moment. He wants the Samaritan woman to learn that she does not have to play "make believe" and just go through the motions of religion. Jesus is calling her to a relationship with him—with God—so that she will be able to live the kind of life God wants for all of us. He challenges her to be a true worshiper who worships God "in spirit and in truth."

- **What is true worship?**

Encourage group members to acknowledge that true worship is not limited to a certain place or tradition. True worship is an attitude of humble, honest response to God. It involves not only hearing God's Word but also putting it into practice. It means giving praise and glory to God not only in a worship service but also in everyday living (see Luke 6:46-49; 1 Cor. 10:31; James 1:22-27).

   b.   *How does Jesus respond to the woman's statements about the Messiah?*

- **What does she show through these statements?**

When the Samaritan woman describes her beliefs about the Messiah, she shows real faith and indicates that she trusts the Messiah will set things right and explain things that God's people don't understand. Note also that she is the one who brings up the matter of the Messiah—another change of topic. She may even have an idea that this man speaking with her might be the Messiah. Nonetheless, she is likely surprised when Jesus says he is the Messiah she's been speaking of.

- **Why do you think Jesus is so direct in revealing his identity?**

As we have noted in earlier lessons of this study, Jesus was not always direct in revealing who he was. Perhaps he is direct here because he knows this is the only opportunity for the Samaritan woman to respond. As we learn later, many other people in her town come to believe in him through this woman's testimony (John 4:39), so he may also have that result in mind.

7. *John 4:27-38*

    a. What do we learn about the disciples from their reactions?

- **What do the disciples need to learn about Jesus?**

The disciples' surprise at finding Jesus talking with a woman indicates that they still don't understand what he is all about. They need to learn that Jesus' love is for everyone, regardless of social status and past experience.

- **What does Jesus teach them about food?**

Again, Jesus sees an opportunity for a teaching moment. The disciples' confusion about the food shows how natural it is for them—like Nicodemus (John 3:4) and the Samaritan woman—to think first of all on a physical level. Jesus explains that the food he is talking about gives satisfaction on a spiritual level that surpasses physical satisfaction. Doing God's will, he says, is the most satisfying food for him personally.

    b. What do the woman's actions and words tell us about her?

Notice that the woman leaves her water jar and hurries back to town. Her excitement is so great that she goes to spread the news about Jesus without further concern for her physical thirst.

- **What would make her so open to telling people that Jesus knew everything about her?**

Jesus' knowledge about her confirmed that he was a prophet. But when he told her he was in fact the Messiah, she suddenly realized that nothing else mattered. This was such important news that her embarrassment about her past life paled in comparison. The arrival of the Messiah meant that staggering changes would soon be affecting everyone and everything.

- **Do you think Jesus' treatment of her, in spite of her past, was also a reason for her excitement? Explain.**

    c. What kind of harvest is Jesus talking about, and what does he say about this to his disciples?

- **What response does he want from them?**

As he speaks about the Lord's great spiritual harvest, Jesus wants the disciples to begin looking at people with spiritual eyes. They probably would have thought of the Samaritan woman as a person least likely to enter the kingdom of heaven. But Jesus wants them to know that God and his prophets and teachers have been preparing a spiritual harvest. This is only the beginning, and Jesus is letting them know they will soon begin gathering this great harvest.

- **Do we sometimes assume that certain people are candidates for heaven and others are not? Why might we do such a thing?**

8. *John 4:39-42*

   What role does the Samaritan woman play in the harvest at Sychar?

She gives her own simple testimony. She tells of her personal encounter with Jesus, and it stirs the people to investigate.

- **What do the townspeople do?**

Despite the character of the woman who'd had five husbands and was now living with another man, the people of the town listen to her. They go to Jesus and urge him to spend time with them.

- **What happens as a result?**

Jesus stays for two days in their town, and many more of the people become believers (John 4:41). Talk about this response in contrast with that of religious leaders who wanted a miraculous sign when Jesus drove the vendors and money changers from the temple (2:15-18).

- **How do the townspeople identify Jesus, and what does that tell us?**

The townspeople accurately identify Jesus as "the Savior of the world" (4:42). Recall together your discussion of John 3:16-17 in lesson 4.

Questions for Reflection

   In what ways are people thirsty today?
   What can we learn from Jesus' treatment of the Samaritan woman?
   How can we let people know what Jesus has to offer?

Explore together and invite group members to pray about ways in which God may be calling each of you to share the good news of Jesus. He offers living water to us all, inviting us to turn to God and be satisfied in his love forever.

Lesson 6
John 4:43-5:47

The Great Healer

Additional Related Scriptures

Numbers 12
Deuteronomy 6:5-7; 18:14-22
Matthew 25:31-46
Mark 2:9-11, 27; 12:30
Luke 13:4-5, 10-17

John 9:1-7; 10:22-42; 11:53-57; 20:29
Acts 5:1-10; 7:20-53; 12:21-23
2 Corinthians 5:17
Ephesians 2:1-10; 4:17-24

Introductory Notes

Our Scripture for this lesson begins with two miraculous healings. Jesus encounters a father whose son needs urgent healing, and Jesus meets a man who has suffered from a disability for thirty-eight years. The religious leaders begin persecuting Jesus because he has healed this man on the Sabbath, so Jesus also takes time to explain his work as proof that he is the Son of God.

In this lesson we also suggest taking time to discuss the purpose of Jesus' miracles. In addition, because the Scriptures for this lesson are lengthy, you may want to note that the closing part of this lesson touches only on Jesus' major points in John 5:16-47. Group members who have additional questions may wish to consult a study Bible or commentary as time permits later.

Optional Share Question

Why is it sometimes more difficult to watch someone you love become sick than to be sick yourself?

1. *John 4:43-54*

   a. *Who met Jesus in Cana, and what was his concern?*

   As Jesus traveled into Galilee and then stopped in Cana, "a certain royal official" came to meet him. Some scholars say this official was connected with Herod, the ruler in Galilee at that time (see Luke 3:1; 9:7-9). This official was also a desperate individual, because he had a son who was close to death.

   • **What kinds of thoughts might have been going through this father's mind?**

b.   Describe the conversation between Jesus and this father.

As you reflect on this conversation, consider that Jesus was addressing a wider audience than just the father of the sick boy. Note also that Jesus had just left Samaria, where the people needed only to hear his words in order to believe. Now Jesus was back in his homeland of Galilee, and he was being asked for miraculous signs. In addition, Jesus had said that "a prophet has no honor in his own country" (John 4:44). John seems to have included this comment to show that Jesus knew his own people wouldn't accept him as a prophet (sent by God to bring God's Word to the people) unless he also showed miraculous power from God.

Notice, as well, that the father didn't seem to want much of a conversation with Jesus. He simply wanted his son healed, so he asked urgently for that. The man also asked Jesus to come to his home, but Jesus didn't go with him.

- **Why didn't Jesus go with the man?**

In this setting, where there was apparently plenty of doubt about Jesus' identity, Jesus may have decided that a test of faith was necessary. It would take more faith for the man (and others) to trust that his son would be healed from a distance than if Jesus went to the man's home and healed the child. To his credit, the man did show that he believed in Jesus' power to heal (4:49).

c.   What was the result, and how did the father respond?

When Jesus said, "You may go. Your son will live," the man "took Jesus at his word" and left (4:50).

- **What does it mean that he "took Jesus at his word"?**

This clearly showed that the father had faith. He trusted Jesus to do as he said.

Some group members may be reminded of a similar healing in which a centurion (a leader of 100 Roman soldiers) asked Jesus to heal a servant who lay paralyzed at his home. In that situation Jesus offered to go and heal the servant, but the centurion, a man who was used to giving orders, said that he knew Jesus only had to say the word and the healing would be done. Jesus praised this man for his great faith and said, "Go! It will be done just as you believed it would," and the servant "was healed at that very hour" (Matt. 8:13).

The case in John 4 had a similar result. On his way home the official learned that his son had been healed. And when he asked what time the

56

- **Why do you think Jesus healed this man at the Bethesda pool?**

You may want to explore this question if group members are curious about Jesus' purpose in this healing miracle. The following "question exercise" may help you lead into a brief discussion about the general purpose of Jesus' miracles:

Some of us might be curious as to why Jesus would heal someone by a pool that people believed was a source of healing. Was it to show that he was the one and only real healer? Perhaps—but if so, why would he heal only one person there? Or might he also have healed others we aren't told about? And why would he heal a man who didn't even know who Jesus was and didn't appear to have faith in him? Wasn't Jesus concerned more about faith than about physical healing?

We probably can't give satisfying answers to any of these questions, but it may be helpful for group members to know that others wonder about some of the same things they might wonder about. It can also help to remind one another that we don't know the answers to all our questions. Our greatest comfort in life, after all, is not found in knowledge but in God through our faithful Savior, Jesus. And while we can know many things about God and about life, we must also trust that God always loves and cares for us, regardless of what we don't know.

- **What was the purpose of Jesus' miracles?**

As we noted in lesson 3 on Jesus' miracle at the wedding in Cana, Jesus' miracles had a twofold purpose: to reveal God's glory and to build faith. Jesus certainly wanted to alleviate people's pain and suffering, but the healing of souls was even more important. One downside of the physical healings he did was that they were temporary; the people he healed would one day get sick again and die. He used miraculous signs to show people who he was, and he sought a spiritual response from them. Miracles were amazing evidence of his "credentials" (see John 14:11); they showed he was the Son of God who had power not only to heal but also to forgive sins (see Mark 2:9-11).

Still, no matter how amazing Jesus' miracles were, they did not ultimately produce faith (see John 10:22-42). Faith is a gift that only God can give (John 3:3). The Lord may use miraculous signs to lead us to faith, but God also produces faith without the help of miracles—and God has worked that way throughout most of human history. Jesus explained the matter this way when he appeared to Thomas after rising from the dead: "Because you have seen me, you have believed; blessed are those who have not seen and yet have believed" (John 20:29).

3. John 5:9b-15

a. Who had a problem with this miracle of healing, and why?

John points out that Jesus did this miracle on the Sabbath, and that meant he would soon have a problem with the religious leaders. They had amassed hundreds of rules about what a person could not do on the Sabbath.

- **Do you think Jesus deliberately healed this man on that day?**

- **Could he have just healed the man and not told him to carry his mat?**

Jesus could have healed this man any day of the week, but it seems he may have had a lesson in mind when he did this healing on the Sabbath. It seems likely that telling the man to carry his mat would provoke controversy. Jesus certainly knew that according to Jewish Sabbath regulations a person was not permitted to carry various things, including a mat. This was not a biblical regulation but part of a code the Jewish leaders had written to "guard" people from dishonoring the Sabbath. The leaders may have developed this code of laws with good intentions, but its legalism distracted people from living by the heart of God's law, which was simply to love the Lord with all their heart, soul, mind, and strength (Mark 12:30; Deut. 6:5). As Jesus pointed out on another occasion, "The Sabbath was made for man, not man for the Sabbath" (Mark 2:27).

If this story provokes a discussion about Sabbath observance, try to focus the discussion on God's design from the beginning—to provide a special time for worship and rest, pointing to ultimate restoration in the new heaven and new earth. To avoid dwelling on Sabbath legalism, it may be most helpful to point out that Jesus' compassion stood in contrast to other people's lack of care about human suffering. On another Sabbath when he had healed a woman who'd been crippled for eighteen years, Jesus said to his opponents: "Should not this woman . . . be set free on the Sabbath day from what bound her?" (Luke 13:16).

b. What happened when Jesus found the healed man later at the temple?

While noting that the man was now well again, Jesus told the man he should stop sinning because something worse might happen to him.

- Was Jesus making a connection here between sin and disability?

From another story we know that Jesus did not associate a person's disability with his own sin (see John 9:1-7). Jesus also rebuked some of his listeners one day when he said, "Those eighteen who died when the tower in Siloam fell on them—do you think they were more guilty than all the others living in Jerusalem? I tell you, no! But unless you repent, you too will all perish" (Luke 13:4-5). Notice that this latter statement is similar to Jesus' comment to the healed man in John 5:14. While God has sometimes punished a person directly for his or her sin (Num. 12; Acts 5:1-10; 12:21-23), we may not conclude that a person's disability, sickness, accident, or tragedy is a direct result of that person's sin. Suffering in this world is a general result of humanity's fall into sin (Gen. 3).

- What response did Jesus want from the man?

Jesus had given the man a new start physically, and he wanted the man to have a new life spiritually as well.

- Why would the man go and tell the Jewish authorities?

Earlier the man had been unable to tell the authorities who had healed him. Now he knew, so he let it be known. Some commentators have speculated that he wanted to please the authorities and get Jesus into trouble. But it's reasonable to conclude that the man simply wanted to give Jesus credit.

4. *John 5:16-30*
   a. *How did Jesus defend his healing of the man on the Sabbath?*

Jesus pointed out that just as the Father never stops working (doing good) in this world, so Jesus never stops working as well. In other words, the universe does not shut down on the Sabbath. God continues to sustain us, hear our prayers, and guide us.

- How did the Jewish leaders react?

The Jewish leaders understood by this that Jesus was claiming equality with God. So they thought he should die for the sin of blasphemy, and they planned to kill him (see also John 11:53-57).

b. What did Jesus say about his relationship with God the Father?

These verses give us a picture of the working relationship of love and honor in which the Father and the Son are linked in purpose. Jesus pointed out that he did nothing except what he knew would please the Father. Because of this relationship, the Father would honor the Son. And whoever did not honor the Son did not honor the Father.

c. Who receives eternal life, and how do they receive it?

- **When do people receive eternal life?**

People who hear Jesus' words and believe in God's message through him receive the gift of eternal life. They "cross over" from the realm of death to the realm of life when they repent and believe. As the apostle Paul explains in 2 Corinthians 5:17: "If anyone is in Christ, he is a new creation; the old has gone, the new has come!" (See also Eph. 2:1-10; 4:17-24.)

- **Where does Jesus get his authority to judge?**

Jesus' authority comes from being one with the Father and having the right to grant life to all who believe. At the end of time all who have believed in Jesus will come out of their graves to live with God forever, and those who have not believed and "have done evil will rise to be condemned" (John 5:29; see Matt. 25:31-46; 2 Thess. 1:6-10; Rev. 20:11-15).

These teachings may be hard for some group members to accept. Listen graciously to any objections, and explain that Jesus spoke these words to religious leaders who thought they had automatic access to heaven and had God all figured out. They should have opened their hearts to see the truth of Jesus' teaching, but were unwilling to listen. People who had God's love in their hearts, however, had already "crossed over from death to life" (John 5:24).

5. *John 5:31-47*

   a. What does Jesus say about valid testimony in these verses?

   b. Why do the religious leaders fail to understand Jesus' identity?

To the Jewish religious leaders, it was important to have a valid testimony. So Jesus gave a logical summary of the examples of testimony about himself. He touched on his own personal testimony, John's the Baptist's testimony, the testimony of the work he was doing, the Father's testimony about him, and the testimony of the Scriptures (often called the law of Moses). The religious leaders, however, believed none of it. They may have believed John the Baptist was God's prophet, but they didn't believe his testimony about Jesus. They did not understand the Father's testimony, because God's Word did not live in them. And although they called themselves scholars of the Scriptures, they especially missed the testimony about Jesus in Scripture because they didn't read the words of God with eyes of faith.

- **Why does Jesus say their accuser is Moses?**

The Jewish leaders believed that Moses was their great lawgiver, the one whom they believed supported everything they said and did. But as Jesus implies, there was a great deal more to Moses than religious legalism. The first five books of the Bible, called the Pentateuch or the Torah, do not simply set up a legal code. They also show that righteousness is the way of trust and belief in the saving grace of God (see Deut. 6:5-7). Moses' life and teaching had pointed to the way of God's grace and deliverance through a future Messiah, and yet the Jewish leaders had dismissed that life-giving message (see Deut. 18:14-22; Acts 7:20-53). The testimony in Moses about God and his love shown in the mission of Christ (Messiah) accused the very ones who called themselves the students of Moses, because they didn't believe what Moses wrote about the Christ.

Questions for Reflection

What do we learn about Jesus from the miracles covered in this lesson? Where do we place our trust?

Lesson 7
John 6:1-24

Power Over All Things

Additional Related Scriptures

Deuteronomy 16:16; 18:14-22   Mark 6:30-56
Matthew 14:13-36   Luke 5:16; 9:10-17

Introductory Notes

The amazing events we study in this lesson show that Jesus has power to meet our physical and spiritual needs and that he has control over nature. How comforting it is to know that no matter what happens in our everyday lives or even when nature seems overwhelming, Jesus is Lord over all things.

Optional Share Question

Have you ever had a time in your life when God acted powerfully to help you or to show you that he's in control? Reflect on that situation and share your thoughts with the group. What were the results? In what ways did that experience strengthen your faith?

1. *John 6:1-4*

    Who followed Jesus to the far shore of the Sea of Galilee, and why?

    A large crowd of people followed Jesus because they had witnessed his healing ability and heard his amazing teaching. In the original Greek text of this passage, John uses the imperfect tense to indicate that the crowds kept on following Jesus and were not about to go away. Invite group members to picture the setting and action of this scene:

    • **Where did Jesus and his disciples go? How did they get there?**

    • **How did the crowds get there?**

    • **What did Jesus do next?**

2. *John 6:5-9*

    a. *What problem developed?*

The crowd would not leave, and before long they would need food. John tells us this happened near the time of Passover, and that meant many people were traveling through the region to celebrate the annual feast in Jerusalem. But there was no food in this isolated place for so many people, so Jesus raised a question about the people's need for food. (This episode in Jesus' teaching ministry is recorded in each of the other gospels as well—see Matt. 14:13-21; Mark 6:30-44; Luke 9:10-17.)

    b.   How did the disciples respond to Jesus' question?

- **Why did Jesus ask this question?**

- **How did Philip respond?**

- **How did Andrew respond?**

Philip responded with some practical thoughts to Jesus' challenge about feeding the great crowd that had followed them. He pointed out that it would take nearly eight months' wages to feed such a crowd. And besides the cost, where could the disciples find enough food for all these people?

John indicates that Jesus was simply testing Philip to see how he would deal with the problem. Philip's answer showed that he wasn't thinking about possible solutions; he was thinking about the impossibility of the situation. Jesus, of course, knew how he was going to solve this problem, but it seems he wanted to do some teaching here about dealing with problems that seemed impossible. Andrew spoke up at this point and said he had found a young boy who had "five small barley loaves and two small fish."

- **Does it sound as if Andrew thought this was enough?**

At least Andrew tried to do something about the problem, but he sounded skeptical about feeding such a large crowd with so little food.

- **Put yourself in the disciples' place at this moment. How would you have responded to Jesus' question?**

3.   *John 6:10-13*
    a.   Describe the steps Jesus took to feed the people.

Jesus had the people sit down, and then he took the loaves, thanked God for them, and distributed them to the seated crowd. He did the same with the fish, and there was more than enough food to go around. In fact, there were twelve basketfuls of food left over.

b. Consider the various details of this event. What do they help us see and learn?

It may be difficult for some group members to grasp the full meaning of this miracle. Encourage everyone to offer their own responses and then mention the following observations if they're not mentioned.

Obviously Jesus' ability to provide abundantly for hungry people is meaningful. In addition, this was a huge crowd. About five thousand men were counted, according to custom in those days—and because all Jewish men were required to go to the Passover celebration in Jerusalem (see Deut. 16:16), this crowd may well have had more men than women and children. But, of course, many women and children were also present, as noted in Matthew 14:21. So there may have been as many as eight to ten thousand people present.

Jesus' offering of thanks reminds us that our food comes from God and that it's always appropriate to thank God for our food. The miracle itself is a statement of God's amazing provision, and it's a reminder of God's provision of manna in the wilderness for the ancient Israelites (Ex. 16).

This miracle also shows that Jesus had the right to call himself "the bread of life" (John 6:35), as we'll discuss in our next lesson. In addition, Jesus later emphasized that the people received "as much as they wanted" (John 6:11). When the crowd had followed him back across the lake the next day, he said, "You are looking for me, not because you saw miraculous signs but because you ate the loaves and had your fill. Do not work for food that spoils, but for food that endures to eternal life, which the Son of Man will give you" (6:26-27).

- **How often do we think of Jesus providing our "daily bread"? (See Matt. 6:11.)**

- **What are some examples of the "daily bread" we receive?**

- **Do we generally receive just enough, or do we have as much as we want, plus leftovers? Why?**

Though probably all of us can point to times when we've been in need, most of us have to admit that we're usually blessed with more than we need—and that includes more than food. Invite group members to reflect on all the blessings they enjoy—and all the needs that God meets by means of those blessings, including the most important one of all: salvation through Jesus.

4. **John 6:14-15**

    a.   How did the people respond to this miraculous sign?

    The people understood that an amazing miracle had occurred. In fact, they began saying Jesus was the Prophet (spoken about by Moses in Deuteronomy 18). This meant that many began to believe he was the promised Messiah. Since this miracle took place near the time of a Passover celebration, nationalistic fervor would have been high. The crowd's enthusiasm was so intense that Jesus knew they wanted to make him king.

    - **What was the people's motivation?**

    Jesus knew the people wanted him to be a political king who would overthrow their oppressors and set up an invincible earthly kingdom. They didn't understand that he was instead the Lord over all kingdoms and powers. He rejected their ideas because his mission was to save people from sin so that they could live and reign with God forever.

    b.   Why would Jesus withdraw to a mountain by himself?

    Jesus withdrew from the crowds because in their fervor over his miracle of feeding thousands of people they wanted to make him a political king.

    - **What would Jesus do when he withdrew by himself? Why?**

    Two other gospel accounts tell us that Jesus went up on the mountainside to pray (Matt. 14:23; Mark 6:46). Another gospel writer, Luke, writes that "Jesus often withdrew to lonely places and prayed" (Luke 5:16). As the Son of God who was not only fully God but also fully human, Jesus often needed to connect closely with God the Father to draw strength and determination for continuing his mission.

5. **John 6:16-21**

    a.   Where did the disciples go, and where was Jesus?

    - **What time of day was it?**

    - **What was the weather like on the lake?**

    The disciples set off in a boat to cross the lake again. It was evening, it was getting dark, and "a strong wind was blowing" so that "the waters grew rough" on the lake (John 6:18). This large lake, the Sea of Galilee, was well-known for its sudden squalls. It looked as if Jesus' disciples were in for a rough trip to Capernaum. John adds that "Jesus had not yet joined them," so he may still have been up on the mountainside praying.

Note: The parallel accounts of this event in Matthew and Mark tell us that Jesus made his disciples leave "immediately" after the feeding of the multitude, "while he dismissed the crowd" (Matt. 14:22; Mark 6:45). As we can see, John's description is different here. If group members raise questions about the difference of details in gospel accounts, it may help to note that this doesn't mean the Bible contains "mistakes." While it may even be possible to harmonize details from different accounts so that they logically fit together into one story, we need to be aware that seamless harmony and accuracy of detail weren't as important to the original writers as we might prefer today. The gospel writers were mainly concerned with sharing the good news of Jesus, and each writer had a particular audience in mind. Inspired by God, they related the stories of Jesus in ways that communicated the good news message effectively to their intended audience. Today we can still share in the good news of these accounts as we accept their central message by faith.

> b.   *What did Jesus do, and how did that affect the disciples?*

When the disciples were a few miles from shore, "they saw Jesus approaching the boat, walking on the water, and they were terrified" (John 6:19).

- **What made the disciples so afraid?**

The disciples were likely already fearful because of the storm. And to see the strange sight of Jesus walking on water in the midst of the wind and waves must have added tremendously to their fear. Mark 6:49 says that they thought he was a ghost.

- **What did Jesus say when they saw him?**

- **How did they react then?**

- **What happened next?**

The disciples seemed to calm down after Jesus identified himself and urged them not to be afraid. John writes that they were then "willing to take him into the boat," and they soon reached the other shore (John 6:21).

Matthew 14:28-31 adds a scene in which Peter attempts to walk out to Jesus on the water. Again, a comparison of the accounts in Matthew, Mark, and John will show some differences regarding location and chronology, but despite variations they appear to cover the same event.

If group members raise additional questions about the Bible's integrity because of these differences, you might note that in real-life courtrooms (unlike fictional dramas), for example, it's considered natural to hear differences in the details of eyewitness testimony. Different individuals don't usually see or interpret a given event in exactly the same way. In fact, suspicions arise when witnesses offer the exact same testimony down to minor details, because it begins to look like they've collaborated on their story. So the minor differences we find in some of the gospel accounts actually lend to the authors' credibility—and thus to the Bible's. When we remember that God chose to give us his Word through imperfect human writers, we can celebrate that all the stories about Jesus in the gospels hold together so well.

If you think it would be helpful for group members who may be struggling with this issue, note further how the important truths of this story emerge from all the accounts—for example, *Jesus walks on water; the disciples are afraid; Jesus calms their fears and brings them safely to shore; Jesus shows he is Lord over nature.*

Remind everyone that the goal of these gospel stories is to give witness to the person and power of Jesus to help produce and strengthen faith. Just as miracles do not have the power to produce faith, neither do the details of stories about miracles. Only God has that power.

So invite group members to ask God for faith and continued strengthening of faith if they have doubts. Jesus wants us all to have faith, and the Holy Spirit is eager to help us grow in faith as we study God's Word to us. We must also remember that whenever we open the Bible, we need to ask for the Spirit's guidance in understanding and growing from it.

    c.   What does this miracle tell us about Jesus?

First of all, it shows that Jesus used miraculous power to walk across the lake instead of walking around it. Second, the disciples witnessed this event and understood it to be a sign of his overwhelming power. He could suspend the laws of nature and walk on water in the midst of a storm.

- **How do you think you might have reacted if you were in that boat?**

6. *John 6:22-24*

    a.   What did the crowd do when they found Jesus was gone?

This crowd was a persistent group of people. Once they found out in the morning that Jesus was gone, they crossed the lake in boats that had come from the town of Tiberias, and they sought to find him in Capernaum.

b.   *What seems to have been their motivation?*

The people wanted more of what they had seen on the mountain. Jesus' healing power and his miraculous feeding of the multitude seems to have drawn them irresistibly to him. Of course, the people were also drawn by Jesus' teaching, but seeing his miracles really got them excited (see John 6:2).

- **If Jesus had asked them for something, do you think they would have been as persistent in following him? Why or why not?**

As we discover in our next lesson, the people grew confused and demanded more miracles when Jesus challenged them to believe in him and serve God. And after he taught about himself as the bread of life, many people deserted him.

- **What is your reason for coming to Jesus?**

Questions for Reflection

Are there any ways in which you view Jesus differently as a result of this lesson? Explain.

What significance does Jesus' power over nature have for us?

Lesson 8

John 6:25-71

The Bread of Life

Additional Related Scriptures

Exodus 16
Matthew 16:23; 26:26-28

Mark 6:52; 8:14-21
John 6:22; 12:4-6

Introductory Notes

It's a part of human nature to want something for nothing. The crowds who had received a "free lunch" from Jesus and had seen his miraculous healing wanted more. In John's original text, the verb tense describing the crowds indicates that the people were continually following him. They were like groupies.

As they interact with Jesus, we again see people thinking mainly on the level of physical needs. Jesus wants them to desire more than physical nourishment. He wants them to search for spiritual food, so he offers himself as the bread of life.

Optional Share Question

Tell about a time when you won something or were given something for nothing. What did you receive? How did it make you feel? Were you surprised by any of the results? Explain.

You can use a situation like this to note that as humans we often want to receive something for nothing. Many of the people in the crowds that kept following Jesus wanted to connect with him at no cost. But Jesus soon taught them that being his disciple could be costly.

1. *John 6:25-27*

    a. What did the people ask Jesus, and what did he say in response?

The people were confused because they knew Jesus did not get into the boat with his disciples the previous evening (see John 6:22). So how did he get across the lake?

- **Does he answer their question?**

We might wonder how they would have reacted if Jesus had actually told them he'd walked on water. Instead he points out that he knows what their motivation is in following him.

- **What motivation would he have wanted from the people?**

Jesus reminds the people that they should be seeking spiritual food, not just physical food. They should be more concerned with eternal life than temporal life. And, he adds, he is the one who can give it to them.

- **What in human nature causes us to be more concerned for temporary things than eternal things?**

b. *What does it mean that Jesus calls himself the Son of Man (see glossary) and that the Father has placed his seal on him?*

Son of Man is a title that Jesus uses quite often in describing himself. He saw himself as the Son of Man in the sense that he was fully human and in the sense that this was a messianic title (see Dan. 7:13-14). In addition, God placed his seal of approval on Jesus at his baptism (Matt. 3:16-17; John 1:32-34), and Jesus is here pointing out that God has authorized all he is doing. If you have time, you might also recall the discussion in lesson 6 on testimonies about Jesus (John 5:33-40).

2. John 6:28-35
What additional questions do the people ask Jesus, and how does he answer?

When Jesus tells the people to work for spiritual food that does not spoil, they want to know what work God requires of them. It's an age-old question. They want to know what hoops they have to jump through in order to get what they want. Jesus replies, however, that it's not a matter of doing; it's a matter of believing in him.

- **What does it mean to believe in Jesus? Is this a one-time event, or do we need to trust him throughout life?**

When Jesus challenges the people to believe rather than to do a mere work assignment, they demand even more of him, saying, "What miraculous sign then will you give?" It's obvious they understand he is asking for a major commitment because they immediately challenge him to prove that he is worth believing in. They show that their true motivation is for physical blessings when they mention their ancestors eating manna in the desert.

(Ex. 16 tells the story of this food God gave the people of Israel while they traveled in the desert after their release from Egypt.)

- **Why are they bringing up that story from ancient times?**

If some group members aren't familiar with the story about manna in the wilderness, it's probably enough to note that the manna was miraculous food God provided so that the people could "be filled with bread" each day (Ex. 16:12). The people who were following Jesus wanted to continue being fed miraculously as well (John 6:34).

In response, Jesus begins with an emphatic phrase that means he wants them to pay attention: "I tell you the truth. . . ." Then he explains that "the bread of God" is a person who "comes down from heaven and gives life to the world" (6:33). In this way Jesus keeps challenging the people to look deeper. Yes, bread that we eat physically might satisfy temporarily. But only the true bread from heaven will ultimately satisfy.

You might also recall that in John 4:15 the Samaritan woman said to Jesus, "Give me this water." Now the people say, "Give us this bread" (6:34).

- **How does Jesus respond to their request? What is he claiming through these words?**

Jesus tells the people he is "the bread of life," and in doing so he uses another emphatic expression: "I am." His Jewish listeners would not have missed his meaning here. This expression clearly echoed the way God named himself when calling Moses to lead the Israelites out of slavery in Egypt (Ex. 3:14). By using this phrase, especially in connection with this discussion about food from God, Jesus is saying he is God.

Note: If you have time, you might also mention that Jesus uses this phrase often throughout the book of John. We'll discuss this matter in more detail in Part Two of this study, when we look at John 14. At this point, though, you could invite group members to explore Jesus' statements in the following passages in a Bible at home: John 8:12; 9:5; 10:7, 9, 11, 14; 11:25; 13:19; 14:6; 15:1, 5. Note also that Jesus used this same expression to identify himself when he walked on water; the Greek text of John 6:20 reads literally, "I am; fear not."

3. *John 6:36-40*

   List the additional things Jesus tells the crowd.

Jesus wants the people to know that because he follows the Father's will, all who believe in him will have eternal life.

- Note Jesus' use of the phrase "come to me." What's the significance of this?

In everyday language this passage explains people's responsibility in connection with God's sovereignty. Jesus calls people to come to him and believe, but he also says that the Father gives these people to him. In other words, people must respond in faith in order to have eternal life, and yet it is God who draws them and gives faith in the first place (see 6:44). This may seem a contradiction, but it's a great comfort to know that God is behind the scenes, calling us to himself. In this discussion it is probably most important to note that Jesus is again promising eternal life to anyone who will believe in him.

- What additional promises do we find in verse 39?

Jesus will not lose anyone who's been given to him. This too is a great comfort for repentant sinners.

4. *John 6:41-51*

a. *What reaction does Jesus receive for his statements?*

The people of Capernaum complain and express their unbelief. Scholars note a similarity here between these people and their ancestors. The ancient Israelites also grumbled against God in the wilderness in connection with the manna God provided for their daily food.

- What method do the people use to discredit Jesus?

They try to discredit Jesus' claim by saying that they know his parents. Because they know he grew up in Nazareth, they say, he could not have come from heaven.

- What point are they missing?

The people are ignoring the fact that they need to listen to the Father and learn God's way. If they did that, says Jesus, they would see the truth and believe in him.

b. *Who can come to Christ?*

Again Jesus says that people must come to him and believe in order to receive everlasting life. And yet no one can come to Jesus unless the Father draws that person. Even so, Jesus emphasizes that the opportunity is open to everyone: "Everyone who listens to the Father and learns from him comes to me" (6:45).

- **How does Jesus know this?**

He knows this because he has been with the Father.

c. *How is Jesus' bread more significant than manna?*

Manna was for physical nourishment, and those who ate it eventually died. The food Jesus offers gives nourishment and eternal life.

- **What does Jesus imply when he says this bread is his flesh?**

- **Why don't the people understand that Jesus is speaking figuratively?**

Jesus is describing his life and ministry as an illustration of bread that can nourish God's people spiritually. We do something similar when we show someone a picture of our family and say, "This is my family." But no one thinks the picture itself is our family.

- **For what does Jesus give this bread?**

Note the connection here between "living bread" and "the life of the world" (6:51). Jesus says he will give this bread so that the world can have life. He will give up the very life that makes him a living human being—"in the flesh"—so that the world can live. Jesus is speaking in cosmic terms about dying to save sinners as well as to break the curse of sin on this world. (See Gen. 3:15-19; John 1:9-13; 3:16-17; Rom. 8:19-23.)

5. *John 6:52-59*
    How does a person have life in Christ, according to these verses?

Again Jesus is speaking figuratively. Unless a person participates in the life of Christ and sees the sacrificial dimension of his life (dying on the cross) given for all who believe, this illustration about his body and blood has no meaning. A person has life in Christ by believing in the power, life, and love of God made clear for us in the person of Jesus Christ. Jesus uses language here that is similar to his words to the disciples at the last supper (Matt. 26:26-28). To eat his flesh and drink his blood symbolizes a believer's total commitment to Christ's life, including his suffering.

- **If you had heard Jesus say these things in the synagogue at Capernaum, do you think you would have been confused? Why or why not?**

Note: Someone may bring up the Roman Catholic view of the Eucharist, which teaches that the bread and wine become the literal body and blood of Christ. To avoid dwelling on differences between various teachings, point out that it's most important and helpful to focus on symbolic meaning in these words of Jesus. Note together that confusion often arose when people kept thinking of literal water, literal bread, and now literal flesh and blood, as Jesus spoke to them. Similar confusion happens today when people give literal meaning to these symbols.

6. *John 6:60-65*

    a. What does Jesus say to those who find his teaching difficult?

The "disciples" mentioned in these verses are all the people who've been following Jesus around, not just the twelve chosen disciples. This large group finds it very difficult to accept Jesus' teaching about total commitment to him.

- **What does this say about Jesus' teaching?**

- **What do you think has been the source of their trouble?**

- **Why have these people been following Jesus anyway?**

Refer back to John 6:2 and 6:26, noting that most of the people in this crowd have been following Jesus for what he could do for them. They could accept the physical food Jesus gave them, but they haven't really been interested in his talk about spiritual food and committing to his mission.

    b. Why does Jesus point out, "There are some of you who do not believe"?

Jesus makes clear that he knows who truly believes in him and who does not. In fact, he has known this from the beginning. There is no way to fool God, who knows each person's heart.

Up to this point, a number of people in the crowd have been playing games with Jesus, pretending to be his followers by tagging along after him. Now he squares off with them and makes clear that he has been speaking about spiritual things, not literal bread and flesh and blood. "The Spirit gives life," he says. "The words I have spoken to you are spirit, and they are life" (6:63). Then he repeats the fact that humbles every one of us before God: "No one can come to me unless the Father has enabled him" (6:65).

- Is this a word from the Lord that we still need to hear today? Explain.

- In what ways might we have to quit playing games and get serious about following Jesus?

7. *John 6:66-71*

   a. *How does Peter respond to Jesus' question?*

The answer Peter gives is one that all Christians recognize at some point. Jesus is the only one we can follow. Peter understands that Jesus is the one who has "the words of eternal life." There is much that Peter does not understand, but he has been with Jesus long enough to know he was sent from God, so Peter knows he has to follow him.

- In your own words, how would you have answered Jesus' question?

   b. *What is said here about Judas?*

- What's significant about this revelation?

John gives his readers a preview here that Judas Iscariot, one of Jesus' closest twelve disciples, will later betray Jesus. (See also 6:64.) This drives home the point that not everyone will follow Jesus, since even one of the chosen Twelve will betray him.

- How does Jesus refer to him?

Jesus describes him as "a devil." It may be interesting to note, however, that Jesus says something similar to Peter on another occasion (see Matt. 16:23). This shows us that even the most sincere of his disciples can fail Jesus at times. Indeed, every one of the Twelve deserted Jesus when he was arrested—and Peter later denied even knowing Jesus. With this sobering scene in mind, encourage group members to examine their own hearts and reflect quietly on some questions like these:

- Isn't it true that any of us could have betrayed or denied or rejected Jesus?

- In what ways have we already done such things?

Questions for Reflection

Do we follow Jesus simply when it's convenient and we can see God's amazing works in our lives?

Under what circumstances might we think it's too hard to follow Jesus?

What keeps us from being unfaithful?

How do we gain strength to keep believing in Jesus?

Close your session with a few words about the comfort of God's care and keeping. Remind everyone that even though we fail our Lord, God is the one who drew us to faith in Jesus in the first place. We can rejoice that Jesus, the bread of life, gives of himself so that we can have eternal life.

If a group member expresses a desire to make or renew a commitment to Christ as the Lord of life, meet afterward to talk and pray together, asking for Christ's healing comfort. If helpful, make use of the "Invitation" and "Prayer of Commitment" provided at the back of this guide and in the study guide.

Lesson 9
John 7

How to Be Unpopular

Additional Related Scriptures

Genesis 17:9-13	Matthew 2:4-6; 9:6
Deuteronomy 18:17-19	Mark 1:22
2 Kings 17:1-23; 25:1-12	Luke 2:1-14, 21
Isaiah 55:1	John 5:18; 6:44-45
Ezekiel 47:1-12	Acts 2
Zechariah 14:8	1 Timothy 2:4

Introductory Notes

The events in our Scripture for this lesson show us that Jesus had to endure a lot of misunderstanding as he brought the good news of God's kingdom to God's people. In this story, which takes place in the context of the great Feast of Tabernacles, Jesus' own brothers present him with a challenge because they do not believe in him. In addition, the crowds express a variety of opinions about him, and the religious leaders aim to arrest him because they want to kill him.

As you study this section of John together, reflect on the challenges Jesus faced in his mission to bring salvation for sinners. He often stood completely alone as "he came to that which was his own, but his own did not receive him" (John 1:11). Even so, he stood strong in the power of God, and in this we can take great comfort, because "to all who received him, to those who believed in his name, he gave the right to become children of God" (1:12).

Optional Share Question

Discuss a situation in which you made a right decision that friends or family members disagreed with.

Explain that in this lesson we see that Jesus sometimes had to ignore the wishes of his family members in order to do what was right. It's encouraging to see that Jesus understands what we go through in this regard, as well as in all the challenges we face (see Heb. 2:17-18; 4:15-16).

1. **John 7:1-11**

    a. *Why did Jesus not want to go to Judea?*

    Jesus knew that the religious leaders in Judea were on the lookout for him and wanted to kill him. Recall a note to this effect in John 5:18 as well.

    b. *Who wanted Jesus to go to Judea, and why?*

    Jesus' brothers wanted him to go to Judea and do more miracles. It was time to go and celebrate the Feast of Tabernacles, and they pointed out that if he was going to be a public figure, he should be doing things in public.

    - **What do you think their motives were?**

    In some ways Jesus' brothers may have enjoyed the attention that came with their family connection to him. Or perhaps they were embarrassed and wanted him arrested (see Mark 3:21, 31-35). They certainly weren't trying to protect him. And they did seem to be challenging him to prove his identity as the Messiah. A key statement in this passage is John's note that Jesus' brothers did not believe in him (John 7:5).

    c. *How did Jesus respond?*

    Jesus said he wasn't going with them because the timing wasn't right. Scholars note that this comment meant he would follow God's timing, not the suggestions of others. Recall that Jesus said something similar to his mother at the wedding feast in Cana (2:4).

    - **What problem might have occurred in going with his brothers?**

    Going with a large group that included his brothers would have attracted attention and given Jesus away. Jesus may also have been concerned for his brothers' safety. Their association with him could have put them at risk too.

    - **What did he do instead?**

    Jesus told his brothers to go without him. Then, after they'd left, he went to the feast "not publicly, but in secret" (7:10). In a text note on John 7:8, the *NIV Study Bible* explains, "Jesus was not refusing to go to the Feast, but refusing to go in the way the brothers suggested—as a pilgrim. When he went, it would be to deliver a prophetic message from God, for which he awaited the 'right time.'"

2. John 7:12-15

a. *Describe the reaction of the Jewish leaders (whom John simply calls "the Jews") when Jesus began teaching at the feast.*

- **How does this compare with other people's reactions about Jesus?**

The Jewish religious leaders were amazed at Jesus' depth and understanding in scriptural teaching. They wondered how he could get such learning without having studied under a recognized Jewish teacher, or rabbi.

Others were also amazed, but their reactions were mixed. Some called him "a good man," while others called him a deceiver.

- **Why were people afraid to say anything publicly about Jesus?**

The Jewish leaders apparently struck fear in most people's hearts. They were the teachers and legal experts of the day, and they were the established authority on interpreting the law for the people. The people also knew that the religious leaders wanted to arrest and kill Jesus (see John 7:25-26). Jesus was a wanted man. So most people would have preferred not to get involved in his predicament—whether they were for him or against him.

b. *Did the leaders' impression of Jesus change as a result of his teaching? Explain.*

There were points in Jesus' ministry when the leaders were genuinely astonished by what he said. But they had determined that he had to be eliminated because his teaching was quite different from theirs, and they refused to consider that he was the Messiah (see John 5:18).

3. John 7:16-24

a. *What do these verses tell us about Jesus' teaching?*

- **Where did Jesus' knowledge and teaching come from?**

These verses show that Jesus' teaching is radically different from that of the religious leaders. People had also said Jesus' teaching was different because he taught "as one who had authority" (Mark 1:22). Jesus explained that his teaching came from the Father (John 7:16); he didn't teach by quoting well-known rabbis, as the religious leaders often did. And he backed up his authority with powerful miracles, as we have noted in previous lessons (see Matt. 9:6; John 4:48; 5:36; 10:38).

- **What would determine whether an individual believed Jesus' teaching?**

Jesus made clear that only a person who wanted to do God's will would be able to believe his teaching. He had made similar statements to the religious leaders on other occasions (John 5:36-44; 6:45).

- **Describe the relationship between Jesus and God ("the one who sent him"—v. 18).**

Verse 18 indicates that Jesus' relationship with God is closely connected and completely united in purpose. Jesus does not seek to honor himself; he seeks only to honor the Father. And since the Father is the source of truth; there is nothing false about the one who works for the honor of the Father.

b. *How does Jesus challenge the religious leaders on their view of the law?*

- **What examples does he give?**

The challenge Jesus makes has to do with keeping the law. The religious leaders are always badgering people about keeping the law perfectly, and yet they do not keep the law themselves. In one example, Jesus says, "Why are you trying to kill me?"—alluding to the commandment that says, "You shall not murder" (Ex. 20:13). He gives another example when he speaks about circumcision on the Sabbath. The Jewish leaders perform the sign of the covenant (circumcision) on the Sabbath to avoid breaking the law, which says a baby boy must be circumcised when he is eight days old (Gen. 17:9-13; Luke 2:12), but they object when Jesus gives a sign of covenant fulfillment by healing someone on the Sabbath (see Isa. 61:1-2; Luke 4:18-21; 7:18-22). In this example, it appears that Jesus is talking about healing the man at the pool of Siloam (John 5:1-18), but he healed others on the Sabbath as well (see Luke 6:6-11; 13:10-17). The problem was that healing as such was not written into the code of rules that governed the Sabbath and was, therefore, considered a violation (see Luke 13:14).

- **Do the religious leaders admit to doing wrong? Explain.**

4. *John 7:25-31*
a. *Describe the confusion that arises regarding Jesus' identity.*

At this point the religious leaders are apparently uncertain about what action to take, and some of the people wonder whether the authorities think Jesus might really be the Messiah, or Christ.

- **Who do the people think Jesus might be?**

They begin to consider that he might really be the Messiah. But then they figure he does not meet the criteria, since they know where he is from.

The *NIV Study Bible* adds a helpful note here, saying that some Jews believed that the Old Testament described the Messiah's place of origin (see Matt. 2:4-6) but that others did not. Different ideas about the Messiah were floating around, and the people did not necessarily agree with their religious leaders on the matter (see John 7:42).

b.   What does Jesus tell the people, and why does he speak so passionately?

Jesus knows what the people are thinking and saying. Without getting into the details of where he was born (in Bethlehem—Luke 2:1-14), he says he is from the Father, who sent him and whose word is true. As a result, Jesus can see that the leaders do not know the Father or the Father's message, because they do not believe in him as the Messiah, who has been sent by the Father to be the Word of salvation for the people. In fact, the religious leaders are so sure of their own view that they do not investigate the claims of Christ. That's why they conclude that he must be demon-possessed (John 7:20).

- **In all the confusion about Jesus, how can some people still believe in him?**

Most people remain confused, but some believe because the Father is drawing them (see John 6:44-45). They ask the right question: "When the Christ comes, will he do more miraculous signs than this man?" (7:31). At least some of the people are getting the message that Jesus is the Messiah.

- **How can we help people get the right message about Christ?**

We can encourage people to consider Jesus' claims as well as the testimony of his miracles. A study of John's gospel can also help give a good understanding of Jesus' claims and his ministry. We can encourage a person to look into all these things, and we can ask God to give that person the gift of faith. We can also draw strength to share the good news of Jesus, knowing that "God wants all [people] to be saved and to come to a knowledge of the truth" (1 Tim. 2:4).

5. *John 7:32-36*

a. *What brought about the attempt to arrest Jesus by means of temple guards?*

The Pharisees heard what people in the crowd were saying about Jesus, and they became convinced that he was getting too popular. The only way to put a stop to that, as far as they could see, was to arrest him.

b. *What did Jesus mean when he said the people wouldn't find him and couldn't go where he was going?*

Jesus was predicting his death and his subsequent return to heaven. "I go to the one who sent me," he said. Again, the people missed his point by thinking in terms of physical locations. They couldn't imagine a place he might go where they couldn't find him.

- **Why would they ask about their people "scattered among the Greeks"?**

The people wondered if Jesus was talking about going to teach other Israelites and their descendants who were scattered far from their homeland after centuries of exile (2 Kings 17:1-23; 25:1-12), but that was mere speculation. Commentator F. F. Bruce points out, though, that in just a few years' time Jesus' message spread and produced faith in many thousands of Greek (Gentile) and Jewish followers throughout the Roman Empire.

6. *John 7:37-44*

Note: Each day during the Feast of Tabernacles, the people performed a water ritual to remind them of God's blessing of rain for the next year's growing season. They used a type of funnel to pour water out over the steps and paving stones of the temple. On the last day of the feast, however, no water was poured out, symbolizing the people's need for life-giving rain from the providing hand of God.

a. *What would be the effect of Jesus' standing up on the final day of the feast to offer the people living water?*

- **What thirst did Jesus want to quench?**

Commentators note that by standing, Jesus drew special attention to his message, because Jewish teachers usually sat (see John 8:2). Some scholars identify this moment as Jesus' official declaration that he was the Messiah, but other passages show that he had made similar announcements earlier (see Matt. 9:1-6; Luke 4:16-21). Nonetheless, Jesus' declaration showed, with a bit of irony, that it was time "to become a public figure," as his brothers had told him earlier (John 7:4). Though his message was figurative and thus confusing to some people, it offered the hope of God's everlasting care and eternal life. Jesus' phrase "streams of living water" reminds us of his conversation with the Samaritan woman at the well (John 4:10-13). It also echoes prophetic statements in Isaiah 55:1; Ezekiel 47:1-5; and Zechariah 14:8.

- **What would those who believed in Jesus eventually receive?**

- **When would this happen?**

John 7:39 states that believers would receive the outpouring of the Spirit of God, and we know this happened on the Feast of Pentecost after Jesus' resurrection and ascension (Acts 2; see Joel 2:28-32). F. F. Bruce adds that some rabbis believed the water ceremony at the Feast of Tabernacles symbolized the promised outpouring of the Spirit on God's people—and they were right.

    b. How did the crowds again show their confusion?

- **Who did they think Jesus was?**

Again the confusion had to do with Jesus' identity. Some said he had to be "the Prophet" (described in Deut. 18:17-19); others said he was the Christ (Messiah). Actually Jesus filled both roles. But others raised questions about his origin. Note that they thought he came from Galilee and did not know he was actually born in Bethlehem (Luke 2:1-14). All this confusion divided the crowd into camps that were for or against him, but at this point no one dared to arrest him.

7. *John 7:45-52*

    a. Describe the experience of the officers who tried to arrest Jesus.

- **How do the religious leaders try to dismiss the officers' explanation?**

There is some humor in this situation as the guards become so impressed with Jesus' words that they simply cannot arrest him. We can almost hear the religious leaders fuming. They resort to mocking what they see as a weakness in the guards. The leaders point out that they do not believe in him, so the guards shouldn't believe in him either.

- **What irony is evident in their statement about the mob?**

The religious leaders claim the mob "knows nothing of the law," and yet they are supposed to be the people's teachers. Ironically they don't see that their teaching has been ineffective. They also don't recognize that some people understand the law better than they do.

b.   *What does Nicodemus say, and why are his ideas dismissed?*

Nicodemus raises a legal question about taking action without having a hearing to find out what Jesus is doing. At this point, however, it seems the Pharisees are beyond reason. They respond by discrediting Nicodemus in a way like they've discredited the guards.

- **What does this show us about Nicodemus?**

Recall that Nicodemus once visited with Jesus and heard the good news message (John 3:1-21). Now, like Jesus, he is pointing out that the teachers of the law are not following the law.

- **What is wrong about the Pharisees' statement about Galilee?**

As the *NIV Study Bible* points out, one thing the Pharisees overlook is that God can raise up prophets from any region or area. In addition, they fail to remember that the prophet Jonah came from Gath Hepher in Galilee (see 2 Kings 14:25; Jon. 1:1).

- **Why do people often try to use personal attacks to dismiss ideas?**

Invite group members to reflect on experiences in which they were personally attacked for their ideas—or perhaps in which they attacked someone else.

- **What are the results of such incidents?**

Questions for Reflection
What were the challenges Jesus faced in his mission to bring salvation?
How can his response help us to face challenges as we bring God's message of love and salvation into this world?

As *The New Bible Commentary* points out, however, while it's possible that Jesus used "currently understood means," there's "no need to assume that he attached superstitious value to them." Other people have gone so far as to suggest that Jesus fashioned new eyes for the man out of the mud he made.

Without delving into wild speculations, we may be able to explain some of the details reasonably. One interpretation suggests that Jesus wanted to challenge the religious leaders on their views of Sabbath-keeping. According to the Jewish leaders, kneading mud was an act that constituted work, so that activity would be a Sabbath violation. We can note also that as soon as the Pharisees learned how the man was healed, they denounced Jesus, saying, "This man is not from God, for he does not keep the Sabbath" (9:16). (Recall, as well, that the religious leaders first objected to another Sabbath healing when they learned that the healed man had been told to pick up his mat and walk—see John 5:8-11, 16.)

- **Do you think Jesus deliberately chose to heal the man this way because it was the Sabbath? Explain.**

The gospel accounts show us that Jesus did a number of miracles on the Sabbath. Perhaps they drew more attention because the religious leaders objected to them. But Jesus' responses often showed that the leaders' views on the Sabbath were inconsistent and confining rather than giving the freedom to do good and to celebrate wholeness and wellness as signs of living forever with God (see Mark 2:23-3:6; Luke 13:10-17; John 5:16-17; 7:21-24). Note also that Jesus could have used only words when he healed the man who was blind, but did not.

b. How did the man's neighbors and others who knew him react when they saw him?

These people saw a man whom they thought was the blind man, but they were confused because he was no longer blind. Some figured he couldn't be the same person they knew, but others said he was.

- **Once the man answered them, what did they focus on?**

After the man insisted that he was the one who was formerly blind, the people wanted to know how he was healed. And when he said that the person who healed him was "the man they call Jesus," they wanted to know where to find Jesus.

- **Why do you think they asked "Where is this man?"**

Point out that we can read this statement in different ways. For example, we might think the people were just curious about Jesus and wanted to meet him. On the other hand, they might have wanted to see if Jesus could confirm the man's story. In other words, they might not have believed everything the man had said. (Note, for example, their demanding tone in John 9:10.)

- **What thwarted them in their effort?**

Like the man who was healed of his disability but did not know who had healed him (John 5:13), the man in this story did not know where to find Jesus.

3. *John 9:13-23*
   a. *What controversy arose when the people brought the healed man to the Pharisees?*

- **Why did they bring this man to the Pharisees?**

- **What was the Pharisees' main concern?**

The narrative does not state why the people brought the healed man to the Pharisees, but it seems likely they were sticklers about the Sabbath law and may well have been hostile to Jesus. Note that the next sentence explains that Jesus had done this healing on the Sabbath. Once the Pharisees found that out, the healing became a religious issue.

- **How were the Pharisees being blind?**

Commentator Leon Morris says, "There were those so firmly in the grip of darkness that they saw only a technical breach of their law, and they could not discern a spectacular victory of light over darkness."

- **What prevents us from "seeing" at times?**

   b. *What did the man who was healed say about Jesus?*

The man was straightforward and stated simply that he believed Jesus was a prophet.

a.   What do we learn about shepherds and sheep in these verses?

•   **How do the sheep respond to the shepherd?**

The shepherd leads the sheep, and they follow. They recognize his voice. He also calls them by name. They know the shepherd's voice so well that they will not be mistaken by another voice and follow a stranger.

•   **In this illustration, who do the shepherd and sheep represent?**

The picture of Jesus as our shepherd is so well known that most group members will make these identifications easily. If the representation isn't clear to someone, though, mention that Jesus explains in the upcoming verses.

•   **Who might the robbers and strangers be?**

Most commentators think Jesus is referring to the Jewish leaders of his day, who, with their many rules and narrow focus on the law, have led many people astray from living God's way. Though we cannot be certain who Jesus' listeners are, it's possible that he is still speaking to some of the Pharisees who threw the formerly blind man out of the synagogue (see John 9:34, 40).

b.   Why do Jesus' listeners not seem to understand his illustration here?

Jesus' listeners certainly know about sheep and shepherds, but somehow they are not getting the message. If any religious leaders are present, they probably can't see themselves as robbers or strangers because of their own blindness to the mission of Jesus (see 9:39-41).

2.   **John 10:7-10**
What does Jesus mean when he says he is the gate for the sheep?

•   **What is Jesus' goal for the sheep?**

Before explaining that he is like the shepherd in his illustration, Jesus identifies himself first as the gate for the sheep. The only way to enter God's sheepfold and thus to be saved and kept safe is through Jesus, the gate.
Other leaders have often misled people to suit their own purposes, but Jesus is the unselfish shepherd who leads and guides the sheep to provide them with God's grace and everything good. He has come to give them life to the full.
Note that Jesus also makes several "I am" statements throughout this chapter of John.

- **What is the thief's ultimate design?**

The thief's goal is not only to take the sheep away but also to kill and destroy.

- **What does it mean to have life to the full today?**

- **How does this compare to other ideas about enjoying "the good life," getting the most out of life, or finding happiness in life?**

- **In what ways are these other ideas misleading?**

3. *John 10:11-18*

   a. *What makes Jesus the good shepherd—and, in fact, the best shepherd ever?*

Jesus cares so much for his sheep that he is willing to lay down his life for them. Anyone who makes a similar claim is a false shepherd who will run from the threat of danger. In the face of crucifixion, one of the most painful deaths ever conceived for execution, Jesus not only approached this kind of death willingly for our sake but also endured it with a joyful expectation in his heart. "Let us fix our eyes on Jesus, the author and perfecter of our faith," says Hebrews 12:2, "who for the joy set before him endured the cross, scorning its shame, and sat down at the right hand of the throne of God." The good shepherd could face his death knowing that the Father would use it to save his sheep from destruction.

   b. *What does Jesus mean when he says he has "other sheep that are not of this sheep pen"?*

Probably the best understanding of this statement is that Jesus is describing people other than Jewish believers. Think of the spread of the good news throughout the world since Jesus' death and resurrection; with his blood he ransomed people "for God from every tribe and language and people and nation" (Rev. 5:11). The promise of forgiveness and full life with God is "for all whom the Lord our God will call" (Acts 2:39). Jesus also spoke of these "other sheep" when he commissioned his followers to "go and make disciples of all nations" (Matt. 28:19).

- **What does Jesus mean when he says, "I lay down my life—only to take it up again. No one takes it from me"?**

Jesus makes clear in John 10:18 that he alone decides to lay down his life. He is not a hapless victim of circumstance. Recall earlier passages in which Jesus said, "My time has not yet come," or in which people could not harm him or arrest him (John 2:4; 7:6, 8, 30; 8:20; see also 8:59). Others may think they're in charge, but only God is. On the authority of God the Father, Jesus would soon give himself up to die and then rise to life again.

4.   John 10:19-21

Contrast the way Jesus' listeners receive his words.

Some respond by saying he is demon-possessed, while others say his teachings are sound and no demon could open the eyes of the blind.

- **What might lead some to say Jesus is demon-possessed?**

This isn't the first time Jesus has been accused of demon possession (see John 7:20; 8:48-52). Because his miracles show he has a source of supernatural power, and because the religious leaders refuse to accept him as the Messiah promised from God, many people conclude that he must be associated with Satan and the powers of evil.

- **What do others say about him? Why can't they write him off?**

While they stop short of confessing Jesus as Messiah, others who are there point out that his teachings make sense—they are not the words of a madman. In addition, he has done good works such as healing a man who was born blind. A demon-possessed man would not do good works or help people.

This group was taking Jesus seriously. Perhaps seeds of faith had taken root, but pressure from Jesus' enemies was keeping these people from expressing their belief in him publicly.

5.   John 10:22-30

Note: The Feast of Dedication is also known as Hanukkah or the Festival of Lights. It's a Jewish celebration of God's deliverance from a Greek ruler, Antiochus IV Epiphanes, who persecuted the Jews and turned the temple in Jerusalem into a place of pagan worship. In 164 B.C. the Jews regained the temple after a bloody struggle led by Judas Maccabeus. Their cleansing and rededication of the temple is still celebrated each year in December by Jewish communities throughout the world.

a.   At the Feast of Dedication what challenge does Jesus receive?

- **What tone is implied in this challenge?**

While Jesus is in the temple area during the feast, some of the religious leaders gather around and challenge him to say specifically that he is the

Messiah. They try to deliver this challenge with a tone of eager anticipation, but he is not fooled by their insincerity. He points out that he has already told them who he is and they have not believed.

- **In what ways has Jesus made clear that he is the Messiah?**

With this question you can invite the group to look back over previous lessons and recall episodes in which Jesus does miracles, gives illustrations, and states plainly that he is the Messiah.

- **Why don't these people believe?**

Referring back to his illustration of the shepherd and flock, Jesus says that the religious leaders and their followers do not believe because they are not his sheep. Only his sheep follow him, because they know and listen to his voice. Recall how the Samaritan woman responded when Jesus told her he was the Messiah; her response was sincere (John 4:25-29). Jesus knows that the people who've approached him don't want the answer he will give them. They've already made up their minds that he is not the Messiah. They simply want him to say he is the Messiah so they can use his own statement against him (see Luke 22:66-23:2; John 5:18).

b. *What does Jesus promise to all who listen to his voice?*

Jesus promises that his sheep have eternal life and that no one can snatch them from him. He reinforces this promise by reminding everyone that the Father has given him these sheep; this means they are also protected by the Father, who "is greater than all."

c. *What claim does Jesus make in verse 30?*

Here Jesus states clearly that he is one with the Father. In other words, he is again saying he is God. Though some interpreters have said this statement does not confirm complete identity with God, Jesus' enemies clearly understood it that way and were ready to stone him for blasphemy—that is, for claiming to be God (see vv. 31-33).

6. *John 10:31-33*
   How do the Jews respond to Jesus' claim?

They see that Jesus is claiming equality with God, so they pick up stones to kill him for blasphemy. According to the law of Moses, anyone who blasphemed was to be executed by stoning (Lev. 24:13-16).

- **What does Jesus say next? Why?**

Jesus asks them which miracle they are stoning him for. In this way he points out that they are being hasty in judging him, because he has clearly taught and shown by his miracles that he is the Messiah, the Son of God (see John 7:31).

- **How do they respond?**

The people wish to stone him because in their minds he is just a man who is claiming to be equal to God and is thus committing blasphemy. Note also that again they show no regard for the fact that they cannot carry out the death penalty.

7. John 10:34-39
How does Jesus answer their charge against him?

Quoting from Psalm 82, Jesus says that if the Scriptures allow people to be called "gods" because they are specially appointed by God—such as kings and judges and other rulers (see Ps. 82:1, 6; see also Ex. 22:8-9, 28; Ps. 45:2, 6-7)—how much more should the one and only Son of God be permitted to call himself God's Son? (See also 2 Sam. 7:14; 1 Chron. 28:6; Ps. 2:7.) Commenting on this passage, James M. Boice points out that the term "gods" in Psalm 82 refers most likely to judges and that Jesus is using a rabbinical argument to support his claim. (This type of argument is often described as arguing from the lesser to the greater.) Judges are given power and authority by God and even function like God in some ways because they pass judgment that can deeply affect people's lives. If imperfect judges can be called "gods," says Jesus, then certainly he can be called God because he is united with the Father.

- **What additional argument does Jesus make?**

Jesus adds that the people should not believe him unless he does what the Father does—again referring to the testimony of his teaching and miracles as the Son of God. Even if the people cannot believe his claim, they should believe his miracles, he says, because they show that Jesus is in the Father and the Father is in him.

- **What do the Jewish leaders try to do?**

Jesus has again argued logically in a way that the religious leaders are accustomed to, and yet they cannot answer him adequately. In their anger they try to seize Jesus, but he escapes. As you and your group reflect on this development, you may wish to note that when the right time comes, Jesus will allow himself to be arrested—but not before (see John 18:4-9).

8. *John 10:40-42*

Why does Jesus go across the Jordan River, and how is he received there?

Jesus leaves Jerusalem and Judea to go to an area where he will be safe for a time. In contrast to the oppressive, calculating religious leaders and their followers in Jerusalem, the people across the Jordan receive Jesus more readily, and many believe in him. Recalling the preaching of John the Baptist in their region, they declare, "All that John said about this man was true."

Questions for Reflection

As you wrap up your discussion of this lesson, invite group members to apply the Bible's teaching personally by asking some questions like these:

Do you believe that the Bible's teaching about Jesus is true?
How would you explain to another person Jesus' teaching about the shepherd and sheep in connection with the claims Jesus made?
In what ways do you hear the voice of the good shepherd in your everyday life?

Be sensitive to Jesus' working in the hearts of your group members. Though some may hesitate to speak openly about following Jesus and putting their full trust in him, they may speak more freely if you take the lead. You can do that by affirming that Jesus, the Son of God, became a human being like us in order to save us from sin and give us eternal life. He promises to guide us faithfully as a shepherd, and because he is God, no one can snatch us out of his hand (John 10:28).

For anyone who may be ready to make or renew a commitment to Jesus as Lord and Savior, an "Invitation" and "Prayer of Commitment" are available at the back of the study guide and on the next page of this leader guide.

An Invitation

Listen now to what God is saying to you.

You may be aware of things in your life that keep you from coming near to God. You may have thought of God as someone who is unsympathetic, angry, and punishing. You may feel as if you don't know how to pray or how to come near to God.

"But because of his great love for us, God, who is rich in mercy, made us alive with Christ even when we were dead in transgressions—it is by grace you have been saved" (Eph. 2:4-5). Jesus, God's Son, died on the cross to save us from our sins. It doesn't matter where you come from, what you've done in the past, or what your heritage is. God has been watching over you and caring for you, drawing you closer. "And you also were included in Christ when you heard the word of truth, the gospel of your salvation" (Eph. 1:13).

Do you want to receive Jesus as your Savior and Lord? It's as simple as A-B-C:

- **A**dmit that you have sinned and that you need God's forgiveness.
- **B**elieve that God loves you and that Jesus has already paid the price for your sins.
- **C**ommit your life to God in prayer, asking the Lord to forgive your sins, nurture you as his child, and fill you with the Holy Spirit.

Prayer of Commitment

Here is a prayer of commitment recognizing Jesus Christ as Savior. If you long to be in a loving relationship with Jesus, pray this prayer. If you have already committed your life to Jesus, use this prayer for renewal and praise.

Dear God, I come to you simply and honestly to confess that I have sinned, that sin is a part of who I am. And yet I know that you listen to sinners who are truthful before you. So I come with empty hands and heart, asking for forgiveness.

I confess that only through faith in Jesus Christ can I come to you. I confess my need for a Savior, and I thank you, Jesus, for dying on the cross to pay the price for my sins. Father, I ask that you forgive my sins and count me as righteous for Jesus' sake. Remove the guilt that accompanies my sin and bring me into your presence.

Holy Spirit of God, help me to pray, and teach me to live by your Word. Faithful God, help me to serve you faithfully. Make me more like Jesus each day, and help me to share with others the good news of your great salvation. In Jesus' name, Amen.

Bibliography

It is our hope that you will have opportunities to encourage members of your group who may be starting their spiritual journey. This bibliography includes some works that aim to help people who may be skeptical about Jesus or who have had little or no exposure to Christianity. Resources like these can help you "give an answer . . . with gentleness and respect" (1 Pet. 3:15).

Barker, Kenneth L., and John R. Kohlenberger III. *Zondervan NIV Bible Commentary.* Grand Rapids, Mich.: Zondervan, 1994.

Boice, James M. *The Gospel of John.* Grand Rapids, Mich.: Baker, 2001.

Bruce. F. F. *The Gospel of John.* Grand Rapids, Mich.: Eerdmans, 2004.

Carson, D. A. *The Gospel According to John.* Grand Rapids, Mich.: Eerdmans, 1991.

Guthrie, D., and J. A. Motyer, eds. *The New Bible Commentary: Revised.* Grand Rapids, Mich.: Eerdmans, 1970.

Morris, Leon. *The Gospel of John.* Grand Rapids, Mich.: Eerdmans, 1975.

NIV Serendipity Bible for Study Groups. Grand Rapids, Mich.: Zondervan, 1989.

NIV Study Bible. Grand Rapids, Mich.: Zondervan, 1985.

Ryan, Joseph. *That You May Believe.* Wheaton, Ill.: Crossway, 2003.

Sayers, Dorothy L. *Christian Letters to a Post-Christian World: A Collection of Essays.* Grand Rapids, Mich.: Eerdmans, 1969.

Tasker, R. V. G. *The Gospel According to John.* Grand Rapids, Mich.: Eerdmans, 1971.

Yancey, Philip. *Where Is God When It Hurts?* Grand Rapids, Mich.: Zondervan, 1997.

Evaluation Questionnaire

DISCOVER JOHN: THE WORD BECAME FLESH

As you complete this study, please fill out this questionnaire to help us evaluate the effectiveness of our materials. Please be candid. Thank you.

1. Was this a home group ___ or a church-based ___ program? What church?

2. Was the study used for
   ___ a community evangelism group?
   ___ a community faith-nurture group?
   ___ a church Bible study group?

3. How would you rate the materials?

   Study Guide
   ___ excellent ___ very good ___ good ___ fair ___ poor

   Leader Guide
   ___ excellent ___ very good ___ good ___ fair ___ poor

4. What were the strengths?

5. What were the weaknesses?

6. What would you suggest to improve the material?

7. In general, what was the experience of your group?

Your name (optional) _____

Address _____

8. Other comments:

(Please fold, tape, stamp, and mail. Thank you.)

Faith Alive Christian Resources
2850 Kalamazoo Ave. SE
Grand Rapids, MI 49560